100 Tips for Hoteliers

Other books by Peter Venison:

Managing Hotels

In the Shadow of the Sun

100 Tips for Hoteliers

What Every Successful Hotel Professional
Needs to Know and *Do*

Peter Venison

iUniverse, Inc.
New York Lincoln Shanghai

100 Tips for Hoteliers
What Every Successful Hotel Professional Needs to Know and *Do*

Copyright © 2005 by Peter J Venison

iUniverse books may be ordered through booksellers or by contacting:

iUniverse
2021 Pine Lake Road, Suite 100
Lincoln, NE 68512
www.iuniverse.com
1-800-Authors (1-800-288-4677)

ISBN-13: 978-0-595-36726-9 (pbk)
ISBN-13: 978-0-595-81147-2 (ebk)
ISBN-10: 0-595-36726-7 (pbk)
ISBN-10: 0-595-81147-7 (ebk)

Printed in the United States of America

This book is dedicated to the memory of Christopher Beaumont, one of the world's nicest hoteliers, who died, before he could enjoy his retirement, on August 15, 2005.

Contents

Introduction

Many years ago, I damaged my back while trying to lift a car, which was stuck in the sand on a beach-development site in Anguilla. This was in the days when there were no hotels or restaurants there and, worse still, not a hospital. As a result, I was flown out to neighboring St. Maarten, bent double and in considerable pain, and transferred to an American Airlines jet to New York, where I was committed to stay in bed, on my back, for two weeks. To relieve the boredom I decided to dictate a book to my daughter, Sue, who at the time, was working as my secretary. The book related some of the experiences I had and some of the lessons I learned in the hotel business. To my surprise, the draft manuscript was picked up by Heinemann, the publisher, and printed almost as it had been dictated. To my further surprise, the book was quite successful, and the publishers reprinted it several times over a few years, until they eventually decided that I needed to replace it or freshen it up. After sending me several requests to do so, the publishers eventually gave up asking and consigned the book, *Hotel Management* to history.

I did not attempt to rewrite *Hotel Management* because, first, I was far too busy at the time and, second, I was just not sure I had anything new to say. Recently, however, I have been confined to a hotel room for quite long periods, attempting to put together an extremely complex business deal involving several South African black-empowered companies. In the waiting time between lawyer's drafts and meetings with the participants, I have experienced the service of a branded five-star hotel, which has led me to conclude that there is still a lot that hotel companies and managers need to do to satisfy the needs of a customer like me. In plain words, I decided that now, I *do* have something to say on how hotels should be run. The result is *One Hundred Tips to Hoteliers*.

I hope this book will be read and enjoyed by all students of the hotel industry, whether they are seasoned hotel managers or young men and women embarking on a career in hospitality. Ninety percent of what I have written here is pure common sense, stirred with a good helping of experience. Recognizing the obvious is, of course, important; being successful, however, means acting upon the obvious. This book is not about theory; it is about action. As such, I believe it will be a useful checklist of things to do for practicing hotel managers and department heads. At the same time, I hope it will provide interesting foresight for those who are just commencing their careers—a taste of the challenges to come and an indication of how interesting and varied a career in hotel keeping can be.

What right do I have, you might ask, to make so many suggestions? Only the right that comes from experience. The tips, or hints, or suggestions included in this book are not hypothetical or theoretical; they come from actual experience—my experience.

I got into the hotel business by accident. By good fortune I had been allowed to take my A-level exams a year earlier than the norm, but I was too young to be accepted into university. As a result, I was asked to stay in high school to take so-called S levels until I reached the magic age of eighteen. Unfortunately, this did not suit my social life, since my girlfriend at the time, as well as all my other good friends, had left school and become people of the world. I did not fancy being a schoolboy any longer.

As luck would have it, a chum of mine had decided to enroll in hotel school, or to be more precise, into the four-year program at Battersea College of Advanced Technology. He suggested that since it wasn't a proper university, they would probably accept me into their course at the age of seventeen. I was there in a flash. After all, I reasoned, I could now tell my friends I was at "college," and, after one year, I could still drop out and go to university. At the end of the first year, however, it was my chum who dropped out (to become an actor) and I who was hooked by the business. Coincidentally, as part of the British government's seeming desire to give everybody in England a university degree, it was announced that Battersea would become the University of Surrey while I was there, and my diploma, rather fortuitously, became a "degree."

When I was nineteen I met another young lady, having been dispensed with by the earlier one, whom I decided I would like to marry. Diana, to whom I am still married forty-four years later, presented something of a challenge. She had been married and came as a package with two little children, Sue and Simon. Upon graduating, therefore, I could not afford to do what the college recommended, which was to join one of the British hotel company's management trainee schemes, because I needed a job that paid sufficiently well for me to do my bit to feed the family. Trainee management schemes, upon examination, seemed to be designed to attract the most intelligent young people in the industry to give as much of themselves as possible to a company in exchange for trainee wages. Instead, I got a job as a desk clerk.

My college lecturers were aghast at my decision to take such a lowly job, just as my headmaster at high school had been when I announced I was to go to hotel school. He had recommended that I pursue a career as a civil servant. There was, however, some method in my madness. The desk clerk job was at the newly opened Carlton Tower Hotel, which was the first American-owned hotel to open in London after World War II and was, for some while, the only American hotel in London. Somewhere, lurking in the back of my young mind, were the thoughts that "getting on" in an American company might be easier, and that I was avoiding the competition by not following the route of everyone else.

The job didn't exactly pay very well; ten pounds per week, if I recall, but the tips were great. Many years later, while entering into a deal with the government in Dubai, I was able to point out to one of the ruling family that this was the second business transaction I had been engaged in with them; the first was to receive a crisp five-pound note every time I handed their father, Sheikh Rashid bin Maktoum, his hotel suite key. Luckily, he came and went quite frequently, and the keys of the Carlton Tower rooms were too heavy to fit conveniently under his Arabian robes.

My instincts about working for Americans also proved right. They were not hidebound by the conventions or traditions of the stodgy (at the time) British hotel industry, where it seemed one would have to be at least fifty to be considered for a position of hotel manager. As a result, after about a year on the front desk, I was promoted to the management services office (something British hotels didn't have) and, thereafter, to hotel assistant manager, then to personnel manager and, after a while, to European personnel director, where my job was to assist with setting up a European expansion program. From this "lofty" position, when the vacancy came up for manager of the Carlton Tower, I was able to suggest myself, and to my surprise, the Americans accepted me. Seven years after starting as a desk clerk at the Carlton Tower, I became manager. I was twenty-eight at the time and the first to realize that this could not have happened if I had been working for Britain's Trust House Forte Group.

From this platform, I decided to be more adventurous. Having met Sol Kerzner, who happened to stay at the Carlton Tower, enabled me to relocate to South Africa with the family (now four children), to become the general manager of Operations for his newly formed Southern Sun Hotels. Ten years later I was deputy managing director of Southern Sun, now listed on the Johannesburg Stock Exchange and the largest hotel group in the Southern Hemisphere. Our earnings had grown at an impressive 20 percent compound-plus for ten years.

Life then took us to the United States, where, together with Oppenheimer Properties, I formed Hotel Properties of America, which operated fourteen hotels in nine states. I also participated in opening one of New York's premier restaurants; was a director of Mandev, an international training company; owned and operated an international sports promotions business; acquired, with others, the site on which now sits Cap Jaluca in Anquilla; developed the Caribbean's first "desert island" for cruise ships; and dabbled with property development in London, before teaming up again with Sol Kerzner to build and open the Lost City at Sun City. This, in turn, led me to return to South Africa, to the position of managing director of Sun International, at the time, South Africa's largest hotel and casino company. My duties included operating a casino company in France and Morocco, managing hotel properties in the Middle East and Indian Ocean islands, and eventually developing the Caribbean's largest resort in the Bahamas, of Atlantis.

Although now retired, I stay close to the business and, as such, am a non-executive director of Tsogo Sun Holdings, currently Africa's largest hotel company, with eighty hotel properties and five major casinos, and a consultant to Emaar Properties in regard to the development of an international chain of hotels by Giorgio Armani.

In case this all reads like a resume for a job application, forgive me. I just wanted to make the point that, along the way, by not following the crowd, I bring to the table a fair bit of varied experience, and this is what I am attempting to pass on through these pages.

The hotel and casino business has been fun—sometimes exciting, never dull, and always hard work! Through it, I have met some fascinating people: kings, queens, consorts, presidents, prime ministers, film stars, actors, writers, politicians, sportspersons, entrepreneurs, and many, many wonderful ordinary folk. I certainly would not have met them in a factory.

The hotel business has taken me to more than a hundred different countries. Through it, I have experienced the horrors and dubious benefits of Apartheid South Africa and eventually participated in the most amazing peaceful revolution in the world. I have also experienced violent revolution in Mozambique, war in Zimbabwe, unrest in Lebanon, communism in China and Cuba, capitalism in the United States, bureaucracy in England, labor strikes in Italy, insurgency in Bophuthatswana, the townships of Africa, the wealth of Beverly Hills, and the unique nature of the French legal system. This is a global industry. You can use it to go around the world or to let the world come to you. If you are thinking of making your career in this industry, it can be as exciting and interesting as you would like to make it.

As I write these words, sitting at a desk in a hotel in South Africa, I notice a logo in the newspaper that is prominent all over the country. It says "proudly South African." It is a motivational logo, probably inspired by the famous "I love New York," which did much to lift the spirits of New Yorkers a few years ago, when morale was low and the streets were dirty. The logo reminded me of something I wanted to say before you read on, and that is: I am proud to have been part of this industry and I hope you will be too.

A few years ago, when our youngest son, Jonathan, graduated from Columbia University in New York, I asked him how many undergraduates were planning to go into the hospitality industry. The answer was none, although one subsequently joined the casino industry and now works successfully in Las Vegas. Most of the undergraduates were going to be bankers. They did not know what they were missing!

1

Choosing the Right Site

Location, location, location—three of the most important words in the vocabulary of business and, specifically, in the hospitality and real-estate sectors. It is obvious that opening an ice cream parlor in the Antarctic or a central heating business on the equator would be senseless. Likewise, operating a Ritz Carlton Hotel in Harlem or an Aman Resort in Blackpool, England, would be a risky enterprise, to say the least. At first glance, selecting a site for a hotel would seem to be a fairly straightforward matter, but there is more to think about than may be readily apparent. It also requires making a decision, which, once the property has been developed, is obviously irreversible. For this reason, it is worth some detailed examination and soul searching before too many checks are signed.

Location is more than just an address. Choosing the right location is full of subtle nuances. I was recently in search of some Ferragamo shoes because I find them comfortable. I am one of those travelers who carry one black and one brown pair of shoes. When one or the other wears thin, I discard them and buy a new pair. On this occasion, I was in New York. I discovered that there were two Ferragamo shops: one in Soho and one in midtown on Fifth Avenue. I happened to be nearer Soho, so I went there. They didn't seem to have much stock and, upon enquiry, I was informed that they had moved the stock to midtown because they were going to close the Soho branch. I was puzzled because Soho is a very trendy part of Manhattan. "That's just it," said the salesman. "It is trendy. But Ferragamo is in the luxury-goods business, not the trendy business." I had never really thought of it that way, and obviously

Ferragamo hadn't either when they opened the store in Soho. Apparently, they found out to their cost.

Tip 1: Don't be rushed.
Decide in haste; repent at leisure.

Mistakes in site selection are often made because the seller is applying sales pressure.

"This is the last decent piece of property left," or "Tomorrow the price will be three times higher," or "If you don't take it, I know that the Hilton guys are in town." We have all experienced this not-so-subtle sales pressure. Ignore it. Do not be rushed. Rather miss an opportunity than make a huge mistake. Selecting or acquiring a hotel site is something that must be done very, very carefully. If the seller cannot give you reasonable time to carry out due diligence inquiries and research, tell the seller that you are not a buyer.

Tip 2: Study the elements.
Look at the trees.

I once tried to sell a beach property to a renowned resort operator. The beach, at Treasure Cay, Bahamas, is spectacular: a long crescent of soft white sand onto which laps brilliant blue (and warm) water. On the day I took the potential purchaser there, the weather was perfect. Upon arrival at the site, he licked his index finger and raised it above his head. "Where does the wind come from," he asked, "and when?"

As it turned out, the reason that the beach was such a perfect crescent was that, for many months of the year, the prevailing winds, light as they often were, blew directly onto it. No matter how much I argued that a gentle cooling breeze ought to be welcomed by sun worshipers, he would not agree; and he was right. Residents might love to be caressed by cooling breezes; holiday-makers, by and large, want undisturbed sunshine.

The elements are important. How can you tell about weather conditions when you check out a site on a perfect day? First, look at the trees. If they are all leaning in one direction, you know where the prevailing winds come from. If they are leaning so far over that their tips are practically kissing the ground, you know that it is too windy, most of the time, to be pleasant. Why do the resorts in Egypt on the Red Sea get such low average rates? One reason is too much wind!

If the beach shows signs of erosion, find out why. You may be in a hurricane belt, or the underwater currents may be dangerous. I was once tempted to acquire a postcard-perfect beach in the Seychelles for a resort development. I could not understand why nobody had snapped it up. I spoke to some of the local villagers. I quickly learned that, on average, two people a year drowned on this beach—and there was yet to be any development on it. There now is, but someone else did it!

In addition to checking out the wind patterns and strength (which can easily be done, because most governments maintain this meteorological data), also check out rainfall statistics. Local governments and real-estate salespeople will always tell you that the monsoon season doesn't really affect their business. Look at the pricing in the tour operators' brochures; that will tell you when it rains a lot. Holidaymakers do not like rain!

I visited Zanzibar on several occasions to discuss a resort deal with the government. Based upon the verbal information, I prepared my financial feasibility model with, eventually, a 70 percent year-round projected occupancy. I then met a man who had once owned a hotel in Zanzibar. He told me that for almost three months per year, it rained so much that he always closed down during that time. Further investigation with tour operators confirmed the point. The resort would have to be almost 100 percent full for nine months per year to arrive at 70 percent year-round occupancy. Governments, since they are made up of politicians, often put a gloss on the truth. Talk to the civil servants with the real statistics, or, better still, to the fishermen who live there.

It is also important to understand the movement of the sun. If your site is a tight one, it may not be possible to build a pool that gets any sunshine. Sun and shade are important elements to a vacationer. If there is not room enough to create a sunny recreational area because it will be permanently in the shadow of your buildings, or somebody else's (either existing or potential), then your resort will fail—or get much lower rates than you expect. And remember, in the Southern Hemisphere, the sun is in the north!

Too much sun (or heat) can also be a problem. Dubai, for example, has developed as a major business and holiday destination. But before you become involved in adding to the already substantial hotel stock there, be aware that for at least four months a year, it is almost too hot to be pleasant. As a result the summer room rates you achieve will be substantially less than those in the cooler winter, for "only mad dogs and Englishmen" go out in the Dubai summer sun. Ditto for Florida.

The elements will obviously affect your design planning. Outdoor restaurants don't work too well in wind, rain, and excessive heat! Air-conditioning bills are higher in hot climates. Water is more expensive in the desert. Ignore these things in your planning at your peril.

Also, take a good look at the soil and the water table. Make sure that you understand what happens to your site in heavy rain. If rivers are nearby, check out the long-term flood data. And talk to the locals about what happens to the sewage systems after big storms; the last thing you want is raw sewage spewing onto your site or into the sea at your beach. And, talking of sewage, if the site is on a beach, and even if the water looks superb, have it analyzed. Sewage can look blue! Also, beware of constructed wave protection devices, such as breakwaters and sea walls. The sea does what it wants to do, not what we want. Check out if the beach has been made with dredged sand; if it has, you can be sure that, sooner or later, the sea will take it back. Protecting your development against natural elements can be expensive. Protecting nature from your development can also be a challenge.

Tip 3: Choose the right neighborhood.
Is this the right address?

If the site seems right, what about the actual location? Is it the right address?

Battersea, London, is only a hundred yards across the River Thames from Chelsea, but a boutique hotel in Chelsea will get high room rates and a boutique hotel in Battersea will probably fail. The natural elements in Battersea are the same as in Chelsea, and the two addresses are equidistant from Big Ben, but they have a different stature and reputation—ditto, Central Park South and Central Park North in Manhattan. They both border the park, but one is definitely at the wrong end. These may seem obvious examples to people who live in or know London and New York, but such things are often not so clear to out-of-towners who have to pick a development site. The dividing line between a good neighborhood and a bad one is often not easy to define. In a city like New York, it can be as narrow as the width of a street or the brow of a hill.

How can a prospective developer find out? Take a walk. Not a drive; a walk. Walk in all directions for several blocks around the prospective site. You will see enough to tell you whether this is a good address or not. Look at the quality and type of shops, businesses, and homes. Are they compatible with your intended business? After your walk, ask yourself if you felt safe. Is this the sort of district in which your daughter could wander alone? Would you let your children come here? Also, get hold of the data reflecting recent real-estate sales. Have they been brisk? Have prices been rising? How long has property been on the market? You can never have enough information, but beware, for much of it will be confusing and contradictory.

Now, take another walk; but at a different time of day and, if possible, on a different day. A beach resort can look very different when the tide is out. What appeared to be a perfect beach at nine in the morning might look like mud flats or a seaweed farm in the afternoon. Try the east coast resorts of Zanzibar, the beaches of the Grand Comores, or even Weston Super Mare when the tide is out. On Wednesday the beach might be deserted, but check it out again on a Sunday, when all of the locals have the day off. Similarly, a city site might seem great at eleven in the morning, but at rush hour the traffic fumes could be deadly.

And while you are there, listen. I once stayed in a hotel in Manhattan that was next to the fire station. Fire trucks in the middle of the night make quite a row—so do ambulances and police cars. On another occasion, I stayed in a hotel next to the garbage-company garage. Same problem: noise. Noise pollution and hotel bedrooms do not mix, so check out your potential neighbors. And bear in mind that the noise will not necessarily be taking place while you are with the real-estate salesman. Have you ever noticed, when inspecting a house you are thinking about buying, how often the seller is playing soft music? That's probably so you can't hear the neighbor's children screaming.

Finally, after listening, do one more thing: sniff! Not long ago, I checked into a hotel in Namibia that was downwind from a seal colony. I had to keep the windows closed.

Different sites, of course, will be appropriate for different hotel products, and in the final analysis, when choosing a site you must know what particular market your proposed hotel will be serving. What price will your clients be prepared to pay and how long will their average length of stay be? Will they be looking for a fancy address or will they be happier next to a convenient highway or airport? Obviously, what is good for the goose may not be good for the gander.

Tip 4: You can make a difference.
Size matters!

If the site is right but the address is wrong, will your development make a difference? Can you, through dint of your building/s, improve the address? That will depend on the scale. That is, the scale of your development versus the rest of the area. If the nearby buildings are all factories, it will be difficult to make a success of a luxury boutique hotel, especially if you are the only one. On the other hand, if your development is of a scale that will dwarf its neighbors, it can make a difference. Anaheim, California, was changed forever by the development of Disneyland. Disney made plenty of landowners in Anaheim very happy with the increased value of their real estate.

It is, however, easier to create a new "address" than to change one, particularly if you can do so on a greenfield site. After Disney's success in Anaheim, its next project was in Florida. Before Disney announced its intentions, it secretly acquired as much land in the area as it could. After Disney World was built, the land value increased dramatically, but this time, Disney, not the neighbors, profited from its own influence.

Sun City, South Africa, is another example of creating an "address." Sun City was built in the middle of nowhere. Twenty-five years later, it attracts almost two million visitors per year and actually features as a real address on most maps of Africa. Real estate in the region sells at high prices. Both of these examples, however, were of such a critical mass and of such a large scale that they had the power to create a change.

Tip 5: Look at the infrastructure.
Don't do desert islands.

The Bahamas has some wonderful hotel sites available on the outer islands. Many of these are far nicer than Paradise Island, Nassau. Why, then, did Sun International build its huge Atlantis resort on Paradise Island? Easy. Infrastructure! Paradise Island is less than half an hour on a reasonable road from the international airport. The international airport is serviced with direct flights from major U.S. East Coast cities and from Europe and South America. The cost, difficulty, and time involved in getting clients from their plane to the hotel are minimal. Hoteliers and hotel developers should not be in the business of providing infrastructure, beyond that required on their own site. That is a job for governments with taxpayers' money. I have been lucky enough to visit scores of beautiful island sites, and tempting as they might be, I have, in the main, left them alone, because the cost of creating the necessary infrastructure of airports, roads, water, and power supply would have been horrendous.

Even if you, or your company, are brave enough to take on the job of creating the infrastructure, be aware that owning an airport does not mean that planes will fly to it. If there are not enough rooms at the destination to warrant scheduled flights, your airport could be empty. Usually, if the product is good enough, airlift will follow, but, if the destination does not offer air carriers enough opportunity to get the right mix between cargo and passengers, or between businesspeople and tourists, you will find it impossible to get scheduled flights. The result will be that your airport will become a charter flight destination, which will lead to the achievable room rates being so low that you may never get a reasonable return on your room investment, never mind on the additional infrastructure. You might also find yourself totally dependent on one or two charter operators, who can always threaten to withdraw service, leaving you high and dry, if you don't oblige them with very low room rates. If you are tempted to buy an isolated beach site because of its beauty, go take a dip in the sea to cool off!

Also, if your site relies on airlift, particularly from overseas, be very careful to examine and understand the restrictions that may be applicable to foreign carriers. Most governments apply stringent regulations to protect their "national" airlines, often to the detriment of their own tourist industry. For example, if London Heathrow will not grant many "slots" to South African Airways, as a favor to British Airways, you can expect that Johannesburg International will not grant too many "slots" to British Airways in retaliation. Another reason the Egyptian Red Sea coast attains such low average room rates is that the Egyptian government forces all international scheduled (not charter) arrivals through Cairo, where passengers must change planes from the foreign carrier to Air Egypt domestic routes. This policy, naturally, forces up the occupancy of Air Egypt (domestic) while adding substantially to the length, inconvenience, and cost of the tourists' journeys.

Wherever your site, beach or city, make sure that your customers, once they are in the vicinity, can actually get to it. Check out the road and other transport systems. Make sure that your prospective entrance is not cut off by a double highway, or a no right or left turn. Make sure the local authorities are not about to charge a toll on your doorstep. Make sure you will be allowed to erect proper directional signage and so on. The Kalahari Sands Hotel in Windhoek, Namibia, is in the best location in the city, but it is almost impossible to arrive by car because of a pedestrian shopping mall and no-parking zones. Some of the best hotels in Positano, Italy, are on a one-way street. If you overshoot the entrance, or there is no room at curb, there is no alternative but to go all around the block, which takes at least ten minutes. If you are considering building in a high-traffic area, give plenty of thought to where the tour buses will park, where the taxis can wait, and simply, how your guests can get in and out of your place with the least distress.

Tip 6: Choose the right site at the site.
Sense the site.

Selecting the right site is one thing; selecting the right position for your development, within the site, is the next. Do not make this choice in a rush, and do not do it only on paper. However large or small the site, get out and walk it. You must "feel" the site. You must understand its undulations, its views, its strengths, and its weaknesses. Take a look at different times of the day. Be there at sunrise. Be there at sunset. Rent a cherry picker and get up in the air, or build a scaffold tower to gauge what the view will be like from the upper floors.

When you think about your planned development for the site, consider how to use the environment and how to avoid abusing it. Tourism can be self-defeating. We find a wonderful virgin site. It is beautiful because it is virgin. We now want others (paying tourists) to share in it, or, some would say, we want to exploit it. There is a huge responsibility not to spoil it. If we do, nobody will want to visit it anymore. There may be great pressure to throw up as many rooms as you can on the site, either from your company for commercial gain, or from the government, which is anxious to create jobs. But remember, you also have a responsibility to your children, at the very least, to build something that enhances, not destroys or spoils, the beauty of the place.

Tip 7: Act on your instincts.
Trust your "gut."

You can check out the foregoing and much more, but finally the site must *feel* right. Just as when buying a house, almost as you walk through the door, you know that this is the place for you; this is the place where you want to live. It is not an analytical assessment; it is a gut feeling. In choosing a site for hotel development, it must feel right in your gut. If it feels wrong and you can't quite figure out why, don't buy it. Your instincts will not often be wrong.

And, two more things! Don't overpay for the land. If the cost of the site exceeds 15 percent of the total planned cost of the development, you may find it very hard to get a good return on your investment, especially in the early days. Next, make sure that the person selling the site has a right to do so. I am, to this day, involved in a dispute resulting from the purchase of a property in Italy almost fifteen years ago. When we wanted to sell the property about five years ago, the real-estate agents put together a very fancy brochure, which they mailed to about 150 prospective high-wealth clients. One of the recipients responded immediately. He claimed that we were selling a property that he owned. It turned out that the original seller had expertly forged the title deeds and sold the property twice!

2

Planning Your Development

Tip 8: Identify your market.
Guess who's coming to dinner?

While choosing the site for a new hotel, you must have some idea of the market you are targeting. If you are working for a company that operates an established brand, then the market for any new development will largely be predetermined.

If you are an individual property developer or hotelier, you will need to identify the market you intend to be in and to decide just how your hotel will be sold. Building a hotel is one thing; letting the world know about it, particularly at the beginning, before it has developed a reputation, is another—but more of this later!

What you build should depend on who you expect your customers to be. Sheikh Ahmed Maktoum, the chairman of Emirates Airline, once told me about a businessman in Dubai who had correctly recognized a market niche in that region of the world to build budget hotels. He had noticed that almost all of the many hotel developments in Dubai were pitched at five-star levels, but that there was a need to accommodate workers, not just bosses. As a result, this man was planning to build rooms measuring seventeen square meters. Sheikh Ahmed had wisely pointed out that although he might fill them in peak season, in the long hot summer, the five-star hotels became very competitive with their prices and many "workers," given the choice of a heavily discounted 45-square-meter room for not much more than the budget box, would opt for the bigger room. The sheikh therefore recommended that the man build rooms of at least 30 square meters to fend off, to some extent, the off-season competition. The man accepted this advice but somewhat missed the point. He also added ornately decorated public spaces to which he could proudly invite his personal guests, with the result that his construction costs exceeded his budget and he targeted neither the five-star nor the budget-hotel market.

Before you put pen to drawing board, it is essential to think through who your customers will be. Will they be on vacation or will they be on business—or perhaps a bit of both? Will they be wealthy or on a low budget—or will they be wealthy **and** on a low budget? Will they be as poor as church mice but having the "splurge" of their lives? Will they be locals or foreigners? Will they be young or old—or will they be young-old? These are just a few of the many questions you should ask yourself before briefing the architect because the answers will dictate the size of the rooms and the scope of the services required.

Whether the hotel planned is a resort or a business hotel (or a mixture of both), it is crucial to decide in which price range you intend to operate. Higher room rates obviously mean higher quality services, which often, but not always, mean more space per customer, better furniture, fixtures and fittings, superior operating equipment, and so on. The cost of building a superior hotel/resort can be over five times higher than a budget hotel or package holiday resort, even though the size of the rooms will almost certainly not be five times more.

Your decision about which market you intend to serve may be predetermined by the company you work for, which could already be in business to serve particular sections of the community and, therefore, will have a clear-cut picture about its customers, both present and future. If you are involved in developing a hotel independently, you will still need to consider, at an early stage, how you intend to market it and how will you handle reservations. Chances are you will ultimately turn to an established chain of hotel operators to manage or market your property, in which case, you will, at the planning stage, be able to tap into all of the knowledge and research that is available to the particular brand involved. Indeed, most branded hotel chains will not only offer advice to prospective hotel developers on the physical planning of a hotel but will actually insist on incorporating certain minimum standards. These standards will run the gamut from room sizes, bathroom sizes, length and height of a check-in desk, the need (or not) for a separate group entrance, the size of the maid's closets, and so on.

Even so, take care. By necessity, most of the branded chains operate on a cookie-cutter basis to greater or lesser degrees. This, of course, expresses itself through standardization, not only with operating systems, which is generally a very useful thing, but also in physical design. This can sometimes be dangerous and inappropriate. For example, I have recently been doing some advisory work for the owners of a large wine estate in the Western Cape of South Africa. They wanted to diversify from wine into tourism and had been entertaining the thought of developing a Ritz Carlton hotel on their land. Having asked the Ritz Carlton people to propose a development plan for a particularly beautiful riverside site on the estate, they were horrified to discover that the recommendation was to construct an almost identical building to the Ritz Carlton in Naples, Florida, a pseudo-Spanish high-rise block. The Western Cape has very strict architectural planning guidelines that generally embrace and protect the Cape Dutch architectural history. Unlike many former colonies, the Spanish had nothing to do with the development of the Cape and it is unlikely, therefore, that the Ritz Carlton clientele would have appreciated "Florida Naples in the Cape," any more than the Capetonians.

You must also consider the size of your property. There is a tendency to cram as many rooms as possible on a site to spread the cost of the land per room, but the more overcrowded a site becomes, the lower the average rate achieved. On the other hand, very small exclusive hotels may be able to command astronomically high room rates, but they need to—because a small hotel requires almost the same management and administrative personnel (i.e., overhead) as one several times bigger. It is not easy to make "small" profitable. An advertisement for a small property costs just the same as an advert for a large one. In fact, it may even cost more because it may need to be in a more exclusive publication. On the other hand, the multiplying effect of a very large hotel on revenues, albeit at lower rates per guest, can be impressive.

Try to plan against obsolescence—the biggest enemy of the hotel industry. Tastes and living standards change. When we built the five-star Saint Geran Hotel in Mauritius in 1973, the bedroom size was 34 square meters (including bathrooms of 10 square meters), and the floors were covered with linoleum. By 2000, the hotel—which had been redecorated several times—was still doing very well but was living on its reputation for excellent service, while most of its international competition sported bedrooms of at least 55 square meters with expansive marbled bathrooms and walk-in closets. Recognizing the hotel was effectively obsolete, we resisted the temptation to redecorate it (again) and, instead, demolished it, replacing it with one that boasted rooms of 65 square meters. The average room rate achieved went from $300 per night to $500 immediately. Had we been able to foresee, back in 1973, that a 10-foot by 10-foot bathroom would be obsolete by the turn of the century, we would have built them bigger and saved ourselves a lot of trouble and expense.

Tip 9: Look around.
What's hot; what's not?

Once you think you have identified your target market, you must decide how to meet its requirements. To do this, you need to understand how others are tackling the problem, and know who is doing so successfully and who is not. You had also better understand the latest trends, fads, and fashions in hotel and leisure facility design because you will need to assess which of these developments will have staying power. This will inevitably require a good deal of research, initially through reading articles, both in the consumer press and within the trade, but also by asking colleagues, associates, and customers about what's "hot" and what's not. To compete successfully, you need to understand your competition; but first, you must identify it. Thereafter, there is really no option other than to go and sample it for yourself; in other words, get out and look around.

When, in the midseventies, my company decided to build a small chain of discotheques to replace some obsolete cabaret dining rooms, three of us, including our selected interior designer, embarked on a seven-day (and seven-night) tour of the world's hottest discos from Monte Carlo to New York to South America. We did not do much dancing but there was plenty of drawing (under the tablecloths) of all of the best design ideas, and the resultant Raffles Clubs were a resounding success. I learned a good lesson on that trip: if someone else is doing something well, don't be afraid to copy it—as long as part of the copying is to modify and improve the idea. And four good ideas from four different venues, when pieced together, take on their own individual character. This is the art of limited plagiarism.

Tip 10: Select the right architect.
Be sure to get the real thing.

The most crucial decision you will ever have to make, in regard to a new hotel/ leisure development, is who to hire as the architect. As in all professions, there are horses for courses. If you are developing a cheaper hotel of the cookie-cutter variety, you will not necessarily need an architect with a lot of flair, but you will need one with a lot of experience and low overhead. If you are developing a more specialized product, where the look and feel of the building are crucially important, you will need to find an architect not only with experience, but also with imagination and exceptional design skill.

Architectural practices that specialize in hotel and leisure work can be located through architectural journals, the Internet, or word of mouth within the industry. If you are involved in developing many hotels during the course of your career, do not think that, once you have found the "perfect" architect, he will be suitable for you to use over and over. Architects develop certain styles, often called "house styles," and while this may be acceptable if you are developing a chain of properties, it is not necessarily going to be appropriate for every job that you tackle.

Having identified the market, you must now identify an architect whom you think can understand what is required. Look for similar properties that have been developed successfully. Find out which architect or architects were responsible. Seek them out. Meet them—not on a neutral site. Go to their offices. Seeing where and how people work gives a lot of clues. Try to gauge the atmosphere in the office. Are people enjoying their work? Does it look organized? And, most important, visit the buildings they have designed. You can get all the books you need from the various Institute of Architects' libraries around the world, but the pictures do not always tell the full story. Nothing beats touching, sensing, and feeling the real thing. When you've touched the real thing, make sure that the architect you are considering was actually the one who designed it. Architectural practices can be large. Often the name on the drawings is not the name of the person that actually came up with the ideas or did the work. And while you are there, talk to the current operators. No one is as well equipped as the incumbent manager to tell you how badly designed the building is! Your choice of architect is a crucial one. The wrong choice—either through haste, lack of information, or just plain bad luck—can be a very costly one.

When you think you have the right person, before you sign on the bottom line, take them to your site. Notice how they size it up. Do they take a cursory look, or do they insist on getting out of the car and walking the whole area? Do they seem excited about the prospect of working on this site—and with you—or is this just another meal ticket? You will want your development team to be riding a passion train. If the architect you have selected is not passionate about the job, nobody else will be.

If your project is big enough, you might want to select the architect through a competition. In this case, make sure to specify exactly what you expect from the contestants, so that when the exhibits are in, you will be able to compare apples with apples. But beware! Most established architects are not keen on competitions to get new commissions. Often, because they are successful and established, they already have too much work on the books to spend speculative time on competitions. If you go the competition route, my recommendation would be to pay for the work done, by all entrants. That way, you do, at least, get their attention.

Tip 11: Then, the interior designer.
You're not just choosing cushions.

Now you will need to find an interior designer and other technical consultants such as structural, mechanical, and electrical engineers, sound and lighting experts, landscape designers, and so on. Your architect will, undoubtedly, have some suggestions. These consultants may be absolutely perfect for the team, but remember that this is *your* team, and although you want everyone to get on well with each other, you also want the necessary checks and balances that a mixture of skills and personalities can bring. The other consultants must be able to challenge the architect, when appropriate.

It may also be important that creativity, as well as practicality, drives the job. It is extremely likely that you will want your building and its interior to be, at the very least, easy on the eye. In this regard, the selection of the right interior design team is very important, and this consultant choice usually comes before others. Don't believe that interior design is something you can do yourself. Interior decorating maybe, but not interior design! Any designer worth his or her salt will not only be highly knowledgeable about the construction, quality, range, and price of all interior furnishings and furniture but should also be capable of architectural and three-dimensional drawing. We are not talking about people who can choose a pink cushion rather than a blue one. We are talking about specialists who can visualize concepts and commit them to the hard drawings that furniture manufacturers, shop fitters, or carpet weavers will use to produce the final commodity.

Once again, choosing the right designer will depend very much on the nature of the job. Don't go automatically with interior designers you have used before; you may have sucked them dry. Interior designers also tend to have house styles, so make sure that the designer's track record is appropriate for the job you have in mind. Also, some design houses are extremely experienced and competent at designing restaurants, others are bar specialists, and others are better at bedrooms than public spaces. Once again, if you do not have a lot of personal experience with various design houses, you can do a great deal of desk research, since most interior designers have never been publicity shy.

However, just as with the architect, don't rely solely on pictures. Get out and visit the real thing. Talk to the people who have had to use the space. See just how good the designer's choice of fabrics was in regard to wear and tear. See how, through public use, their layouts have been modified. See whether the enterprises they designed have been successful. Then, find out exactly who worked on the jobs you have looked at. Large design firms have many designers. Your job will only be as good as the personnel who work on it. It is no good selecting your design firm based on a particular project it has done, only to find out that the designer who worked on it has left the company and started up on his own elsewhere. And, when you think that you have found the interior design firm that you like, make sure that the designer is compatible with your chosen architect. Both will be "artistes." Both will have specific roles. But, they must be capable of respecting each other.

Also, don't believe everything they draw. Most interior design firms will employ renderers to draw pictures of the planned finished products. Check these drawings carefully against the reality of the actual space available; sometimes too much artistic license is taken. And, in these days of computer drawings, much of what used to be done by hand is now done by machine, and such machines are not always too clever at placing tables and chairs in future restaurants. Machine-drawn restaurant layouts have difficulty understanding the view. Sometimes, they don't focus on how people actually sit on chairs. If diners had to sit on the chairs that have appeared on some plans I have discarded, they would have had their stomachs on their plates.

Tip 12: Establish a road map.
Let the budget rule.

You can select the rest of your planning team according to less subjective criteria. At the minimum, you will certainly need good structural, mechanical, and electrical engineering advice, so you might as well hire these professionals as part of your team from the beginning. In selecting these consultants, make sure they are experienced at the type of job you have in mind. These consultants will readily supply you with a list of projects that they have worked on. Factual checks in this area are easy to achieve.

You will need to consider how you are going to manage the design team. Make no mistake, the management of the design process is a full-time job. If you are not able to do it yourself, it is essential that you appoint a project or development manager; someone who is experienced enough to keep the "artistes" in check and on budget. The budget, per se, will be the essential tool that your project manager will utilize. To establish this budget, you will need to use the services of yet another professional, a quantity surveyor. This person will be able to take the initial conceptual ideas and space plan from the architect and measure the probable quantities of materials and time that will be needed to turn these ideas into reality. Initially, of course, the measurements will be broad brush, but as the drawings and ideas are refined and re-refined, the quantity surveyor will be able to produce harder and harder numbers, until eventually, before any construction takes place, these numbers can be translated into a firm construction budget. For this reason, I am a great believer in having this professional as a permanent member of the development team, attending every planning meeting and, eventually, every site meeting during the construction phase. It is precisely the quality surveyor's line-by-line costing that forms the actual budget; this is the road map you will use to navigate your way toward the end of the project.

Tip 13: Visualize—everything!
Get operational input.

Your development team is now complete, bar one essential element. With the exception, maybe, of you, no one on this team is actually going to operate the end product. They will, during the planning process, be constantly seeking guidance from the operator or hotel management. Or, you hope, they will! It is, therefore, essential that the development team include an operational specialist, who may, in turn, need to seek additional guidance from others such as chefs, maintenance engineers, housekeepers, and so on. Obviously, it is important not only that the project eventually look right but also that it function properly. More often than not, these two concepts are not compatible! Your operational specialist will need to examine every line on the drawings. This person must be able to visualize the plans in three-dimensional form and to challenge their practicality from every angle. This is an extremely detailed and time-consuming task; there are no short cuts. The operator must study every nook and cranny of what is proposed. What will this door bang into when it is wide open? What happens in this corner where these two walls meet? How can you open these windows? How can the customer reach those bath taps? Where can we hang or store the towels? How do we clean under that bed? How does a guest get from the restaurant to her room in the rain or in the dark? Won't that air conditioning blow straight at the bed? Can you hear the people in the next room? Is this room big enough for two queen beds? Are the chairs drawn in the restaurant plan the right size? How can we fit in some round tables? How can the guest read such small letters on the phone handset? What do you see when you sit in the bathtub? Can I see over the balcony railing when I sit in the chair? A thousand questions, each one as important as the last, but each one, in its own way, a minor piece of the puzzle. Never was there a truer saying, in respect to hotel development, than "the devil is in the detail."

Timely operational input to the development team is a big job. Make sure that you, or the person responsible, have the time and experience to focus on it properly. If you decide to use a management company to do this work, don't shortchange them. If they are to do it properly, they will need to be paid for it. Make sure, as well, that the management company sees your development as unique. Don't allow them to fob you off with their solutions to the last job. Even when you are involved with cookie-cutter design, it is rare two jobs are exactly alike, due to the particular topography of each site. In room design, it is possible to replicate over and over again. In public areas, it is far more difficult, unless, of course, you are working for McDonalds.

Tip 14: Let everyone feel proud.
Teamwork at work.

For this reason, it is important that an operator is present from very early in the planning process. In fact, a key to the success of the plan is to have all participants on the team as part of the process from the outset. In this way, the number of changes that have to be made are minimized because everyone will have had an opportunity to speak as things come up for discussion or the opportunity to raise questions. In this manner, everyone buys into the concept and detail of the project; everyone feels a piece of ownership of the project; everyone can be proud of what is being planned and built. There will always need to be tradeoffs between desirability of design and cost, between image and practicality. Settle these arguments as part of the team process; get them behind you and move on.

Tip 15: Hike the site.
Touch it, feel it, understand it.

I cannot stress enough how important it is to use your site well. To do this, you must really know it. This knowledge cannot be gained from site plans alone nor by walking the site without proper contour maps. There is no substitute for trampling all over the site with a decent map in hand. This will give you the opportunity to see exactly what is there; to see what would be good to keep and what would be good to remove. For example, the site may include some fabulous trees that, either you will have difficulty getting permission to cut down, or you would be crazy to do so, because they add so much to the ambiance. Or, the site may have some wonderful rock formations that are not obvious from the site plan, but that would be either very expensive to move or unwise to do so in terms of visual impact. Either way, you had better understand what stays and what goes because your architect is going to have to design around these elements.

It is also vital to understand, not only what your potential buildings will look like from offsite, but also what you can see from the site. I have frequently been lured to visit potential hotel sites by developers who sent me pictures of the site and its wonderful beach, only to get there and realize that the most prominent view from the beach was an oil refinery or a local shantytown.

Sometimes, there is absolutely nothing you can do about such eyesores, which means that someone probably chose the wrong site in the first place. In most instances, however, the worst aspects of the view from the proposed hotel can be mitigated by clever building design and placement. The only way that you can make these judgments is onsite, and you must take into consideration, not just where you are standing but where you might be standing in the completed building. It will probably be necessary to build some scaffolding towers to ascertain what, exactly, a potential guest will be eventually looking at from hotel bedroom windows, bars and restaurants alike. In some cases, a 10-meter move to the left or the right can make a huge difference to the end product.

It is also possible that the site itself offers such overpowering opportunities that you could never pick up from the plan itself. Maybe the noise of the waves crashing on a particular rock, or the nesting birds in some trees, or the way the sunset filters through the landscape, or whatever, can make the difference eventually between a good project and a spectacular one. The only way to decide this is to know and understand your site better than the back of your own hand.

Tip 16: Draw before you pour.
Finish the plan first.

Having identified your market, examined your site, and selected your team of consultants, you should now be in a position to become much more definitive about the project, to a point of deciding its scope and shape, including the size, range, and style of the proposed facilities, such as restaurants, bars, retail, and so on. This, in turn, might dictate the need for more specialists before you can finally brief the architect (for example, if you decide to include a Japanese restaurant, you might want some specialized input from outside your team), but more detailed planning can often take place once construction has commenced.

It may be necessary for you and your team to come up with a unique concept for the project, unless the concept is dictated by the brand. Whatever the concept, it is important to understand the habits of your potential guests and to plan to accommodate them. For instance, pay heed to the fact that the human race seems to have certain herdlike tendencies. People like to meet people, or, at the very least, people like to watch people. That is why such ancient concepts as the Galleria in Milan, or the Champs-Elysées, or Leicester Square attract so many people. There is a buzz about these places that draws people to them. If you are planning a resort, keep this principle in mind. Don't spread your restaurant and bar facilities all over the place. Rather cluster them around a focal point, a sort of village square, to create a center of activity and excitement. By all means, create a couple of quiet spots, but don't expect your guests to have fun (and spend money) there. "Buzz" in our business is important. Whether you are designing a city hotel or a resort, you will need to find a way to create the buzz. And remember, for some reason people like to go down to nightclubs and up to restaurants. And, multilevel casinos don't seem to work as well as those on a single level. And, hotels with a sense of arrival work better than those that don't have it. Hotel pools, particularly if people are clustered together, seem to be more popular than beaches.

In an ideal world, you will complete all detailed design before you put a spade into the ground. We do not, unfortunately, live in an ideal world, and the financial pressures to get the job done often mean that one has to design and build on the "fast track." Whereas this may be unavoidable for various reasons, it is not normally desirable, because unfinished design work will inevitably lead to unnecessary change as construction continues, and change orders to builders can be very expensive indeed. The simple rule is that the more complete the design process is before construction commences, the more definitive a builder can be about the price for the job and, as a result, the more you, as the developer, will have control over the costs. In other words, draw before you pour—the concrete, that is.

Tip 17: Make a model.
Three dimensions are better than one.

No matter how desperate you are to start the construction and finish with the planning, always commission a model of your proposed building. Initially the model can be a very simple one, built of cardboard or balsa and positioned on a contoured site-representative base. As conceptual design proceeds, other more detailed models should be commissioned of such a scale that you can actually get a three-dimensional feel of the proposed building/s. Don't be afraid to build larger-scale models of crucial parts of the project. Such models are fantastically helpful in defining the shape and scope of your project. They bring to life the concepts of the architect in a way that almost everyone can relate to. They stimulate comment and controversy. They help you understand the bulk of the buildings in a way that one-dimensional plans can never do.

Models are invaluable. Rather spend fifty thousand dollars on a bunch of scale models than fifty million building the wrong thing.

Tip 18: Keep contingency budgets.
Blueprints don't have eyes.

Finally, keep this in mind. No matter how careful you have been with your planning, you must keep an open mind to the possibility of change during the construction phase. Nobody can think of everything, and it is certain that, as the building/s emerge from the ground, other good improvement opportunities will become apparent. You will realize, as you stand in the concrete shell of your new lobby, that a certain pillar is blocking a particularly good view, or you will realize that if you could route the driveway to the front door ten yards to the right, that the arrival impression will be improved 50 percent. These are the type of things that will happen and that you will want to correct. To do so, you must have planned for change, which means that you must have budgeted for it. Whatever your well-planned budget is, add 10 percent for contingencies. You will certainly need it!

3

During Construction

Tip 19: Set an end date.
Timing is everything.

Decide when you want to open the project to the public. This decision will be driven mainly by the builder's program but can be fine-tuned in accordance with business needs. As a general rule, the quicker you can build and open the property, the sooner you will be able to start generating cash, as opposed to just spending it. However, this decision must be a balanced one, taking into consideration a complex cocktail of information.

Construction time lines are, to a large degree, dictated by circumstances beyond your control. For example, cement takes a certain time to dry, and a good tile layer can only lay x number of tiles per hour. However, in theory, ten tilers can lay ten times more tiles than one; and two shifts of workers per day/night ought to get twice as much work done as one shift, provided of course that they can avoid the wet cement. Normally, the speed at which a job can be completed is in direct correlation to how many bodies you can throw at it. Overtime and night shifts are expensive, so you will have to weigh carefully the costs of rushing a job against the savings gained from finishing quickly. Also, keep in mind that whereas, in some parts of the world, workers may be in plentiful supply, supervisors and consultants may not be—and supervisors will need to get some sleep, if they are to keep supervising efficiently.

Very often there will be some external needs that decide the construction time line. For example, if you are building a resort hotel in the United States in Florida, it would be better to open it to the public at the beginning of the winter tourist season, rather than at the end. Some resorts in the Indian Ocean make more money in the period from Christmas to Easter than they do in the entire rest of the year. In these circumstances, to finish building in May would be a crime.

Also, as far as resorts are concerned, it is important to understand the tour-operator brochure printing schedules. In some countries, these important marketing tools are only printed once per year. If you miss the deadlines, you can lose a lot of business. Remember, in many places it is illegal to show a rendering of what a building will look like in a travel brochure; you have to show the finished product (or a finished part of the product).

There may be other influences, such as an upcoming major international convention or an event such as the Olympic Games, that dictate when you should open the project; from this date, you can count back, taking into consideration the preparation and training time the operations people will need in the building once the construction crews have left. These issues will dictate the optimal time for opening the project; then you will need to do some detailed, analytical work with the construction company and your quantity surveyor to see if such timing is practical.

The worst thing you can do is to leave the finish date floating. Decide at the beginning which date you are going to open and stick to it. Nothing concentrates the mind better than a ticking clock. Everybody needs goals and targets. Such undertakings without end dates are meaningless; they never seem to get finished or achieved. You will be amazed what is possible when everybody focuses. For example, I have previously mentioned the rebuilding of the Saint Geran hotel in Mauritius; it is a good example. The decision was made to demolish the existing hotel and to rebuild on the same site at about the same time a decision had been made by the new owners of the Sandy Lane Hotel in Barbados (a distant competitor to the Saint Geran) to do the same. The existing Saint Geran was still profitable, particularly during the winter season. The optimal time for it to be closed was between Easter and Christmas, effectively seven and a half months. Also, the success of the existing Saint Geran was very much due to the levels of service, and that, naturally, related to the "software," the personnel. It was essential to retain these personnel during the closed period, which meant that they would have to be paid during the downtime. To incur this expense for more than one low season, as well as missing a peak season's trading, would have rendered the whole exercise far too expensive.

Also, to envisage opening a new hotel (hardware) without the well-tested software, was stupid.

There was, therefore, little choice but to plan to demolish the existing hotel, build a new, infinitely better one, and reopen it with the same staff, in the period between Easter and Christmas. This decision demanded meticulous planning before construction commenced. It also dictated the sort of negotiation that took place with the construction companies, which had to commit to the task or suffer huge penalties. With everybody in agreement, and thoroughly focused, the job was done. The old hotel was removed and a 180-room, state-of-the-art replacement, complete with three new restaurants, was up and running, with all of the grass and trees replanted around it, in less than seven months.

Meanwhile, in Barbados, the Sandy Lane took more than three years to be rebuilt. During that time, many of its clientele came to stay at the new Saint Geran and never went back!

Tip 20: Pay frequent site visits.
See how it grows!

The key to successful construction is for the person ultimately responsible for the project to visit the site frequently. When Sol Kerzner was building the original hotel at Sun City, in the middle of "nowhere," about a ninety-minute drive from his office, he decided that the only way to keep the project on time, and on budget, was to visit the site almost every day. That way he didn't get too many surprises. Since more than three hours of driving every day was out of the question, Sol bought a helicopter (which he sold for a profit when the job was finished!), which he used almost every morning for a fifteen-minute flip up to the site before breakfast and before the office opened. That way, it was impossible for the construction company to fool him about progress. Not that he could cover the entire site before breakfast, but since he was selective about the areas he visited and did not announce beforehand where he was going, the builders never quite knew where he would look next.

By visiting frequently, even as a "lay" person, it is possible to monitor progress. For example, if a wall is being built, you can note carefully where it has reached on day one and compare this to where it has reached on day two. It is then very easy to figure out whether the amount of bricks laid during the intervening day was reasonable. If you try to figure out the progress of the wall after three weeks, it is more difficult to pin down whether progress was reasonable or not. This sounds rather elementary and obvious, but amazingly, most developers just don't do it.

Also, catching something as it comes out of the ground, so to speak, gives you the chance to change it early if it is obviously wrong, or if, now you are actually on-site, you can see a better solution. Changing direction before too much damage (and expense) has been incurred is smart. Changing things that are obviously wrong, however far they have developed, is essential, but only before the project has been opened. Once the business is up and running, it is very hard to close down (even parts of it) to make the necessary corrections. Often it is too late. I will never forget flying over the Beacon Island Hotel with Sol Kerzner in a small plane about two weeks before the (fully booked) hotel was due to open. The gardens had been completely landscaped and a brand-new oval swimming pool sat proudly in the center of the lawn.

"Shit!" exclaimed Sol, as we circled and recircled over the building. "We've built the pool in the wrong place." With that we landed and sped to the hotel site where Sol, to the amazement of his project manager, instructed the builders to rip up the newly finished swimming pool, while he took out a piece of paper and started drawing a free-form rock pool, similar to one he had seen in a magazine the day before. "But we only have two weeks to go before the hotel opens," whined the project manager. "And think of the cost we've wasted on the pool we've built."

"Never mind that," instructed Sol, "if we don't do it now, we never will." He was right. That's what contingencies are for. And, in addition to that, all of the new guests commented on how innovative the hotel rock pool was, even if they couldn't use it for the first two days of their stay.

The other big benefit of visiting the site frequently during construction is that the workers get to know how passionate you are about their work—and passion is contagious. You also get to see for yourself, which workers and supervisors know what they are doing and are prepared to work hard. You get to know the straight shooters and the ones who are not. This is important. When the chips are down, and you need to make a big thrust to get the job finished, you know, and can insist, which supervisors and their teams to put to the task. You also get to know what is happening on the ground. As a result, it is difficult for the construction company to bullshit you. Most disorganization on a building site is due to incompetent planning by the managers or late delivery of plans from the architect. Neither the architects, nor the construction company, will tell you that; but the workers will.

The workers are not fools. If they can see that the boss works as hard as they do and really cares about what they are doing, they will move mountains to please him. There is huge pride on the job on a construction site. Mostly, it is not harnessed. An owner, walking the site, can go a long way toward doing so, especially if he occasionally reaches into his pocket and offers a little personal reward here and there.

Tip 21: *Construct through communication.* Hold regular site meetings.

During construction, it is vital to keep communications and information flowing. It is no good if the developer issues instructions for change at the shop-floor level. This must to be done through the right channels. It is, therefore, essential to respect the chain of command, or chaos will ensue. It is also essential to hold regular site meetings on a highly structured basis and in the presence of your planning team. Such meetings are needed to review progress on the job, as well as for a reality check against time and budget. It is vital that the minutes of these meetings are properly recorded, and that all decisions and action steps are circulated to the appropriate people, on a need-to-know basis.

Although everyone involved must be party to the progress and decisions regarding change, it is possible for the agenda to be compartmentalized to avoid uninvolved parties wasting time. For example, there is not much point in including the landscape consultant in the meeting about the kitchen equipment, and vice versa. Nevertheless, the project manager and the quantity surveyor must be present for all sections of the site meeting in order to maintain control. The careful organization of these site meetings is extremely important. Although it would not be sensible for them to be open ended (because the subject matter in meetings always seems to expand to the time available), it is important to allow ample time for each item on the agenda to be fully explored and addressed. A great deal of detail is dealt with at these meetings, detail that gets more and more voluminous as the job moves from broad-brush concepts to shop fitting and final finishes. A great deal of interaction should also be taking place between the operations and the development teams, for it is at these meetings that many, often irreversible, decisions need to be taken that can affect future operations for the life of the project.

For this reason, it is as important for the executive responsible for operations to continually walk the site as it is for the developer. It is often the case that what an operator approved on paper a few months earlier does not stand up to the test when it is actually built. Or indeed, that what is being built is not what was operationally approved. The best way to mitigate these errors is to catch them early, and the only way to do this is by "being there." Good operational input is vital, but it must be given with regard to the construction time line. It is not very clever being wise after the event. A smart operator will be wise before, or even at, the event; which means that he had better be ready with the right input at the right time.

It is also crucial to ask the quantity surveyor to revise and update the budget continually to incorporate the changes that result from decisions taken in meetings or on site. Only by knowing exactly how the project stacks up against the budget can change decisions be properly made.

Tip 22: Build a mockup room.
See it, touch it, feel it.

Just as it is essential to build three-dimensional models of the project during the period of conceptualization, it is very important, and useful, to build a mockup room (or rooms) once the detailed design work and selection of materials has been completed, but before it has been finalized. At this stage, it will be too late to change the basic dimensions or location of the rooms, but within those parameters, there is plenty of scope to examine the choices that have been made about the interiors before purchasing commences. Mockup rooms can be built in low-rent space, such as garages or warehouses, conveniently near the decision makers. They need not be built at the development site, particularly if the site is a distant one. It is essential, however, that the mockup is built to the exact size, shape, and dimensions of the real thing. What it looks like from the exterior is unimportant; but internally it must represent every detail that has been designed in regard to wall and floor surfaces, fittings and fixtures (for room and bathroom), furniture (both soft and hard), light fittings and switches, air conditioning and heating controls, colors, textures, and so on. The complete mockup should spark considerable comment from all involved, regarding the "feel" and ambiance of the room. Is it striking? Is it comfortable? Is it warm? Is it "cool"? Often it is a good idea to ask comments from potential guests, or others from the appropriate market sector, who have not been involved with the design team. Both practical and subjective comments should be taken on board and considered.

It is equally important, however, that the operations team take the time to examine the detail of the planned room from a far more practical point of view. Now is the time to take every item in the room and question it. Why do I have to get down on my knees to open the safe? How do I turn on the taps in the shower without being scalded? Aren't the taps on the sink going to be difficult to clean? How can I change the light bulbs? Why does this door bang into that one, when fully open? Why are there so many unsightly wires behind the bedside table? How do I turn the lights out when I am in bed? Where are we going to store the throw cushions after the turndown service? Why are the drawers so shallow? Or, why aren't there any drawers? Why are the lights above the mirror not bright enough to apply makeup? Where is one supposed to hang the towels? Look at the awful view I get when I sit in the bathtub? Why can't I see the TV screen from this chair? Why is there so little hanging space in the wardrobe? Why can't I see over the balcony when I sit in the chaise lounge? And don't think that one person will spot everything. If you already have your maintenance chief on board, he will have a completely different set of comments; your housekeeper will have others. In fact, at this point, the more the merrier because nothing has been bought. Ultimately, however, someone will have to make some decisions, because the comments will be far from unanimous, and these decisions will, of course, need to be a sensible balance of style, cost, and practicality. Most people who have been invited to comment will understand.

Tip 23: Don't shop without a list.
Line-by-line precision.

Whereas a great deal of broad operational input is required in the preconstruction phase, it is during construction that most detailed operational planning will take place, such as that described earlier. So, by definition, it is always "fast track." It would be expensive and unreasonable to stop construction while the "operator" figures out what is needed. Once again, budgets play an exceptionally important role in operational planning. The budgets, which can be carved out of the master project budget and are likely to fall under the control of Operations, are normally the Operating Supplies and Equipment Budget, the Pre-Opening Operations Budget, and the Pre-Opening Marketing Budget. Each of these budgets will need to be prepared on a line-by-line basis, incorporating every item of expenditure that is envisaged before the hotel actually opens. This process requires a painstakingly detailed examination of the proposed operations, taking the planning far beyond the broad concepts decided upon in the preconstruction period.

Tip 24: "Walk" through every operational area.
Everything and the kitchen sink.

To construct an Operating Supplies and Equipment Budget, each operational area of the proposed project must be "visited" and examined, and every piece of equipment, large and small, must be itemized and budgeted for. This process will require management upfront to decide on operating criteria, and for this reason, it is probably sensible to include in the operational team, at this stage, the person who will be responsible for opening the hotel in due course. Such operating criteria will, of course, be influenced strongly by the overall concept and standard set by the developer; nevertheless, each item will have to be thought through from an operational point of view before a budget can be set. For example, before you can decide how many sheets will be needed, you will have to decide how many king, queen, and twin beds are in the mix. This figure will, in turn, depend on the potential market for the hotel and on the operators' understanding of that market and their sleeping habits, which are not always easy to work out. How many couples like to sleep in the same bed? How many couples are expected, as opposed to singles, irrespective of how they like to sleep? How many couples traveling together are not really "couples"? How many conventions do we expect, where unrelated couples will be sharing the same rooms? How much single occupancy do we expect? Then it will be necessary for decisions to be taken on how frequently linen is changed. Will we use duvets or sheets and blankets? What quality linen shall we use? How full will the hotel actually be? How quickly can our laundry turn around the sheets? Will we actually have our own laundry? Each of these things will need to be debated, decided on, and then transferred onto a schedule, which will eventually translate into exactly how many types and quantities of each piece will be required, and how much they are expected to cost. And that's only bed linen!

Similar thought will need to be given to each food and beverage outlet, starting with menus and bar lists. Only when you have decided what is going to be served, can you decide on how it is going to be served and from what it is going to be eaten or drunk. Having done so, each item must be quantified and priced. There are, of course, thousands of items! And every single one requires a decision.

The Pre-Opening Operations Budget primarily involves payroll, inclusive of recruitment and training costs. Detailed assessments will need to be made of exactly how many staff, both management and support, will be required in each department of the proposed hotel, how are they to be recruited, how will they be inducted and trained (and at what cost), and often, as a result, how long will they need to be on the payroll before the opening of the project? Staff can, in the main, be broken down into two major categories in regard to pre-opening: those who are needed to plan the opening and those who are needed to participate in it. The planners, by definition, will need to be on board earlier. Those who are essential to establishing operational criteria will be needed as much as a year before opening, as well as those responsible for planning and carrying out the recruitment and training program. Each position will need to be identified and entered into the pre-opening budget as a function of the projected salary and the number of weeks each person is to be on board prior to the hotel opening. Each pre-opening budget will differ in accordance with the size and scope of each project.

Tip 25: Choose people with passion. Mix them up.

One of the biggest costs covered by the Pre-Opening Operations Budget is recruitment. The complexity of this exercise depends on the location of the project. Obviously, if you are opening a hotel in a First World metropolis, such as London or Paris, there will be a large pool of trained labor, provided the development is of interest to prospective recruits. On the other hand, if you are trailblazing, by opening an hotel on a remote Third World island, where you are only allowed to hire local inexperienced islanders, you may have a large pool to choose from, but, alas, one in which nobody has the first concept of what will be required of them. Or, alternatively, you might be opening up in a place like Dubai, where hotel work is not on the wish list of any local inhabitants, and you are obliged to recruit every last worker from overseas, especially if there is a ban on poaching from existing hotels, as there often will be.

Whereas all of these scenarios will require a different approach to the logistics and planning of the recruitment exercise, one thing should remain constant: The people you need to become your employees (and representatives of your company to your guests and clients) should *all* have the overriding desire to be of service, not only to your customers, but to each other. It is no use hiring the most skillful waiter in the world if he is surly, and it is no use hiring the best sauce cook on the planet, if she can't get on with the vegetable chef. In other words, the qualities you should be looking for, during your recruitment campaign, are those associated with a friendly disposition, combined with the will to work hard for others.

When we were recruiting staff for one of the first luxury hotels in Mauritius in the early 1970s, there was no pool of skilled, nor experienced, staff to fish in. We placed an advertisement in the local paper requesting applications from candidates, who would receive appropriate training, for the following positions: cooks, waiters, receptionists, housemaids, and accounts clerks. We had 2,000 long-winded letters of application for the 200 positions we had available. Of those, 1,800 of the applications were for the position of accounts clerks. We started by interviewing the 200 who weren't. While the applicants were waiting outside of the interviewing room for their turn, we asked them to fill out a questionnaire. It invited them to tick off what would be their favorite job from a list of non-hotel jobs, in the event that they had the opportunity to do other work. The top choices were consistently teacher, police officer, or male nurse. The first two had much to do with status; the third, it later became apparent, was because the British government had a shortage of hospital cleaners in England and was willing to pay fares to import this menial labor.

We also found, during the actual interviews, that most of the applicants had never worked, even though there was an acute shortage of workers to harvest the island's sugarcane. "Why," we asked, "have you not worked in the fields?" The answer was always the same: "Because I am educated!" We did not hire many of the first batch of applicants. However, ultimately, we did locate enough candidates who had worked in the fields, so to speak, and were keen to commence on the bottom rung of a new career. We also looked for the most outward going of these, which was not always easy to assess in a one-on-one interview, when the candidate can feel extremely intimidated. Years later, I found a better way to interview candidates in small groups. In this method, questions are thrown into the vacuum of the group. It soon becomes apparent which candidates have the confidence to take a lead, which ones are overbearing, which ones are accepted by and acceptable to the others, which ones help each other, and which ones have an "attitude."

It may also be important to hire a good mix, if such a thing is possible. For example, don't hire only Pakistanis for the accounts department, and Filipinos for housekeeping, no matter how strong your preconceived ideas are about the natural talents of Pakistanis and Filipinos. The organizational chart of hotel staff already contains plenty of barriers to efficiency and difficult interfaces. Don't aggravate this by creating extra cultural barriers between the cooks and the waiters, or between the desk clerks and the housekeepers. Do your best to create a cultural melting pot, which should become the unique culture of your hotel. It is unfortunate, but to a degree it is true, that good-looking, fit, tidy, well-groomed, healthy staff are better suited to the hotel industry than unkempt, fat, dirty, untidy ones. But remember, good looks can be in a smile or a twinkle in the eye, rather than an hourglass figure. I was once visiting the national hotel school in Cuba, which was attached to a functioning hotel and restaurant. While in the dining room with the principal, I could not help but comment on the attractive wait staff. "That is because," he explained with a big grin, "all of the ugly ones are in the kitchen! You couldn't do that in the great United States of America!" He was right, but the food was lousy.

Tip 26: Open full throttle.
Plan to be busy.

The third and final element of the Pre-Opening Operational Budget is marketing. There is, of course, no use in building a hotel or leisure development if you don't let people know that you are doing so. The trick is to let the right people know for the least possible expense. You can wait until the place is ready, but absolutely the best way to open any new hotel business is to open it at full tilt. There is a very strong school of thought, from the universe of hotel managers, that hotels should be weaned up to full occupancy, thereby giving the new staff time to adapt. I am completely opposed to this approach. In my view, it is much more sensible to open up at full steam or as full and busy as you can possibly be. It is incredible how quickly staff can learn to cope and adapt. The danger is that if they start slowly, they never get to be quick. The only way you have any hope of opening with a full house is by premarketing the product. By definition, that means marketing funds have to be spent from a pre-opening budget, which must be very carefully devised and which will be discussed in more depth in later chapters.

4

Getting Open

Tip 27: *Don't delay the wedding.*
Opening is a target.

There is one very important favorable dynamic to opening a hotel; that is, the fixed opening date. By fixing the date (and sticking to it), the whole process becomes extremely task oriented. It's like getting ready for a wedding. There are lots and lots of things for brides (particularly) to do, but somehow they get done, because the date is cast in stone. How often have you heard of a wedding being delayed because the cake wasn't ready or the bride's shoes didn't fit? Not many! Somehow, everything is done on time because there is a very firm deadline to meet. Divorces, on the other hand, seem to rumble on unpleasantly forever.

I cannot stress strongly enough how important it is to set a realistic date for opening a new hotel and to abide by it. The target date makes everybody focus, from construction crews to cooks. It's a bit like taking exams. When I was a kid we only got one shot at our eleven-plus exam or our O levels and A levels, so we had to study in an increasingly urgent fashion right up to the examination day. Recently, I was discussing one of my grandson's impending exams, because he didn't appear to be taking the deadline for revision too seriously. "Not to worry, Granddad," he explained, "if I don't pass it this time, I can take it again after Christmas." You only get one chance to open a hotel, so you better be ready, and everybody in the team better know it.

If you are the leader of the operational team and are ultimately responsible for getting the project functionally prepared to open on time, your task is clear. There can be no doubt about what the goal is. Your role is to assess the multitude of things that need to be accomplished, break them down into bite-size pieces, allocate appropriate resources of both people and money to each piece, closely monitor performance, and bring in reinforcements when required. It is also your job to delegate the responsibility and authority to each task leader, to be available and flexible to plug the gaps as they appear, to keep your eye on the target, to remain calm, when everyone else might be panicking, to compromise your set standards only when you have absolutely no other choice, and to work just that bit harder than everyone else.

If you are also responsible for the project management (i.e., getting the hotel constructed on time), then you definitely need to delegate the operational side of opening to another. There are three clear functions to be performed in getting a hotel open, once it has been designed: (1) building it to the right standard, on time and on budget; (2) having sufficient trained personnel, equipment, and supplies to open it efficiently; and (3) marketing and promoting it effectively. These three roles are highly interlinked, particularly the first two, as are the last two, but they are so complicated and potentially overwhelming that three separate team leaders are normally required.

Tip 28: Remain flexible.
Expect the unexpected.

As the operational team leader, you will constantly need to be aware of the progress your project management colleague is making, and the state of the building, because, piece by piece, he or she will hand it over to you. Although you will have agreed on a schedule for this to occur, it will not always happen in the order you had hoped, and you will, therefore, need to remain very flexible and cooperative. For example, you have agreed with the project manager when the staff canteen will be available, which should, of course, be early enough for you to start feeding your new recruits and trainees. From the project manager's point of view, under pressure, however, the staff canteen might become less important to finish than the guest dining room and, given the choice of one or the other, you could probably understand his position. Nevertheless, the staff needs to be fed, so contingency plans have to be made and upset chefs have to be placated. One thing you can be sure of; with a building project, not everything will work out as planned or scheduled, and constantly arguing about it, rather than solving the problems, as they occur, will not make matters better.

Another thing to be prepared for is that something major and completely unexpected will go wrong. I have been directly involved in opening more than twenty hotels and all of them delivered an unpleasant surprise. In one hotel it was a water supply problem, in another it was sewage, in another it was a construction strike, in another the baths were impounded by customs, in another the workers were always drunk, and in one, the pristine beach became a haven for man-eating fish. You can't always forecast what will go wrong; just know that something will and that you must deal with it as best you can at the time.

Tip 29: Have a plan, and then have a backup plan.
Go to plan B.

The key to everything is to have a clearly delineated plan. It's like using a map to get from point A to point B. Although the map doesn't tell you where the road works are, or where there are deviations, if you find, for whatever reason, you have to change your route, at least you can tell from your map where to rejoin. If your operational plan lists all of the tasks that need to be achieved and takes cognizance of the approximate time they will each take, given the resources allotted to them, you can monitor progress quite easily and move your resources around. If you start to see that your resources are too limited to cope, then you can always make a backup plan. It may be possible to bring in reinforcements from other parts of the company or, if they are not available, from labor agencies. It is strange that if there is well-paid work to do, you can find someone to do it. Or indeed, if, for example, a particular section leader or supervisor is falling down on the job, there is often someone else right under your nose, who might even be one of his employees, who can step up to the plate. When you start to fall behind in the journey because someone is not coping, or the relevant supplies are being delayed, what you must not do, under any circumstances, is nothing. Your job, as team leader, is to forecast trouble and to have the backup plan ready. By closely monitoring and continuously reviewing the progress of your section leaders, you will normally know, before it is critical, if things are coming unglued. At that point you must be prepared to act, however painful the decisions might be.

Tip 30: Prioritize your involvement.
Concentrate on what can't be changed.

As team leader, you must also prioritize your personal involvement. To some extent, this will depend on the relative strengths and weaknesses of the people you have hired to get the job done, almost all of whom will probably be going on to run the hotel, or parts of it, once it is open. One good plan is to get more involved personally with all decisions that will have long-term effects and less involved with decisions that can be changed more easily in the light of operational experience. For example, it would be smart for you to be involved in the choice of most operating equipment, especially those pieces that affect the overall image of the place. You are much more likely to be in tune with the design concepts than, say, a newly hired restaurant manager, because you will have lived with the project since its inception. The choice of a teapot, for example, might seem relatively unimportant, but you won't want to toss out all of the teapots the day after opening (having focused, retrospectively, that they are the wrong ones) because they do not contribute to the overall tone of the place. This, in fact, holds true for most operating equipment, big or small. On the other hand, the decision as to where the hotel buys oil or bananas has such a short-term effect that it would be an unwise use of time to get involved.

Plenty of items also seem to fall into the crack between the project management and operations teams. If you are not careful, no one pays attention to them until it is too late to make good decisions. For example, signage often falls into this category, as do uniforms. Both items seem to be so simple, but they are not. There are absolutely no short cuts for signage. Apart from the image impact of signs, both large and small, from the neon hotel sign on the roof to the door numbers, every single one has to be thought through and determined to be correct. Only someone with an intimate knowledge of the layout of the building and who is completely in tune with the design concepts can do this job. In my view, it is one best tackled by the operations team.

Tip 31: Pick the right batting order.
Get operational management on board early.

It is highly likely that the first employee to be hired will be the hotel manager. A full year before the opening date is not too early. It is only right, since the rest of the team will be reporting to him, that he should be involved, and indeed decisive, in hiring them. The choice of hotel manager is crucially important. However, it often presents a problem because of the completely different role that an "opening" manager plays to an "ongoing" manager. Over the years it has become apparent to me that the skills involved in organizing the opening of a hotel are different than those required for managing it on a day-to-day basis. Perhaps *skills* is the wrong word; it would be more correct to recognize that the nature of an opening manager is likely to be different from the nature of an ongoing one.

Opening a hotel requires an organized mind and a calm, cool hand. As stated before, there is a very clear goal in sight, one that doesn't take much explaining. Also, there are no hotel guests to complicate the issue, although, naturally, many decisions need to be taken with guests in mind. That, however, is not the same as having to put interaction with hotel guests as your top priority. A great hotel manager will interrupt any internal management meeting to step outside to meet and greet a guest. An opening hotel manager doesn't have to do this. On the other hand, an ongoing hotel manager doesn't have to spend hours poring over blueprints or inventing the hotel operating systems or visualizing how things could be; what she has to do is continuously motivate her personnel to operate the systems day after day after day, to the same high standard; she has to keep reinventing new mini-goals to stretch her employees. There is not one all-consuming, mighty goal. It is worth, therefore, giving consideration, if it is practical to do so, to the concept of an opening specialty team, just like American football clubs have a special kicking unit.

The second hotel employee to come on, should, in my view, be the hotel controller or accountant. It is important that the manager is involved in his selection, but it is also important that he be given a large degree of autonomy. His role will be to take charge immediately of the design of all financial reporting and control systems as well as their implementation. He will quickly need his own assistants because, as soon as is practical, he will be required to take charge of the control of large sums of money involving the pre-opening budgets, especially in regard to the constantly growing payroll and the purchase of operating equipment.

Shortly thereafter, the team will need to be augmented by the other key divisional heads, specifically, the food and beverage manager and the rooms division manager, together, as early as possible, with an executive chef and a housekeeper. It is also very helpful to bring on at an early stage the maintenance engineer. His understanding of exactly how the building has been designed, and actually works, from a mechanical point of view is of paramount importance, especially since most hotel managers are greenhorns in this area. By being around as the mechanical systems are installed, there will be much greater likelihood that he will understand and agree with their design and, therefore, far less likelihood of him wanting to change them all as soon as the hotel is open. On so many occasions, I have witnessed a team of professionals set up systems (e.g., lighting or heating control systems) at great expense and with great thought just to have them instantly overridden by some "handyman" maintenance engineer, three weeks after the opening, because he doesn't understand them or doesn't like them.

Tip 32: Hone in on the head count.
The mass recruitment plan.

The other crucial member of your top team will be the human resource director or personnel manager. He or she will be the quarterback for the mass recruitment and training function, which will need to be coordinated across all departments. There is no point, for instance, of the food and beverage manager rushing off to, say, Mumbai, to hire waiters, if Mumbai could also be a fertile recruitment ground for chambermaids. The plan for mass recruitment and, thereafter, training needs to be fully coordinated to be efficient and cost-effective.

The first thing for the newly assembled management team to work out, in this regard, is how many workers will be required and what their conditions and pay will be. To do this, of course, the team must set the standards of operation and, as a result, the levels of service to be offered and the caliber of staff required. This is a long, detailed, and grueling exercise, which probably cannot be completely achieved before the first mass recruiting has to begin. However, certain broad and fundamental decisions can be taken, which will affect staffing levels and standards dramatically. For example, it will take more maids and housemen if a decision is made to turn down guest rooms in the evening; and, it will take more waiters if twenty-four-hour food and beverage room service is to be offered. When planning an opening in a foreign country, take great care to understand the myriad of public and religious holidays that will affect your staffing schedules. Also, take careful note of any other government regulations that will impact you. For example, in recently planning the operations of a mega resort in Marsa Alam on the Red Sea, I was surprised to learn that all employees to be hired from Cairo would have the right, by legislation, to return home (at the hotel's expense) for one week every month.

Staff housing will also need to be considered. In a major metropolis with good public transport systems, this should not present much of a problem. However, in many parts of the world, an up-market hotel or resort is often located in an area where staff accommodation is too expensive, and transport from cheaper districts is not available. The logistics, in this regard, will have to be studied and solutions found before staff counts, or the nature of the shifts to be employed, can be finalized.

Other considerations will be the levels of business forecast, particularly in regard to the seasons and expected business cycles, as well as the natural drop-out from the first batch of persons employed. It would be unusual to find that every single employee hired either actually shows up on the day or fits in. You can expect a large percentage of no shows and early dropouts; the size of that percentage will depend on the quality of your selection process. It makes sense, therefore, to over-recruit at the beginning, to compensate for the drop-out factor.

You must also decide how flexibly you can staff the business. In certain locations and countries, there is a pool of labor readily available to tap into as the need occurs. For example, in the average Holiday Inn in America, the staffing of the front desk and housekeeping department is organized on almost a daily basis, according to the level of bookings. A few core (permanent) employees are augmented daily, either from agencies or from a list of part-time workers, such as students, to whom temporary and part-time work is appealing. In other instances, and in other countries, where the employment of unionized employees is problematic, many jobs can be contracted out to third-party companies that are not subject to the same union-negotiated rates or other regulatory encumbrances. Both of these strategies may appear to be cost-effective, but management will have to consider carefully the effect on service standards. Training and disciplining somebody else's employees to handle *your* customers is not so easy!

Tip 33: Question and answer.
Conducting the interviews.

Having decided how many staff you need, in what categories, and at which levels of skill, you are almost ready to recruit. What you still have to do is to decide exactly the starting date of each position. This decision will depend largely on the planned readiness of the new building. There is no point in having too many staff, for too long, in theoretical classroom-type training. They need to be in the actual surroundings where they will be going to work, touching, and feeling the actual equipment. Don't, therefore, bring the masses on too early, because you can take poison on one thing; the building will not be ready on the date, or in the order, that the builders or the project manager have promised. The only date that resonates with them is the day the guests are going to arrive, not the day the staff is. Also, no matter how much classroom training you manage to achieve, nothing beats the on-the-job training that new staff get, when it involves *real* guests. Nothing focuses the minds of your new trainees more than when they have a guest to deal with rather than a role player or trainer.

That is not to say that you should not plan any classroom training and staff orientation. Of course, you must. But be aware, that a lot of the things you teach will change in the light of actual operation, a lot of the people you are teaching will drop out, and of those who don't (the majority, you hope), many will go blank when they are confronted with their first real paying guests. I have often sat in on classroom-training programs, where the trainees had learned by heart the price of every drink in the bar, and how to mix every cocktail in the book, only to witness them "freeze" and forget everything when confronted with the pressure of actual live service. Obviously, a good way to overcome this problem is, as soon as is practicable, to conduct dummy runs with "guests" from your other hotels (if any), from travel companies, from suppliers, and so on. This is not without cost considerations, because you will not be charging these guests, but it is as close as you can get to the real pressure that your staff will have to face. At the same time, it can be a very good public relations exercise.

If, of course, you are in the fortunate position of opening a hotel in a location where there are already many other operating competitors or a huge pool of trained staff to draw upon, then much of this will not apply. In these cases, it is important to spend as much time as you can, as early as possible, visiting the competitors, and picking off the best people that you observe—if you can afford them!

Where there is not a deep pool of local talent to draw on, it will be necessary to spread your recruitment net wide. In so doing, you should try to avoid recruiting all the staff from the same place. You do not want a hotel in London to feel, due to a propensity of staff from one area, that it is in the Philippines, or India, or Italy, or wherever. Similarly, try to avoid staffing one department with any particular national group. There are enough natural barriers to communication in a hotel organizational structure, without aggravating them by having all Indian accounts clerks and all Italian waiters.

In regard to the actual interview planning and techniques, remember, when interviewing supervisory staff, not to tackle too many candidates in one day. Make sure that the interviewers write up each candidate immediately after the interview. By the end of a day of back-to-back interviews, it is very difficult to keep one candidate separate from another. When you conduct an interview, maintain a high level of alertness and concentration. Since it is likely that you will be asking many different candidates the same questions, it is sometimes very easy to lose concentration and not listen properly to the answers. This, obviously, is a complete waste of your time and the candidate's. Use leading and open-ended questions that encourage the candidate to do most of the talking; for example, "How do you feel about your last job?" rather than "How long did you work there?" will encourage the respondent to talk. First impressions are very important because, for some jobs, it could be the same first impression that your future guest will get. Note physical features or mannerisms that will later remind you of which candidate was which; this will help you, at the end of each tiring day of interviews, to reflect quietly on which were the best candidates.

Finally, remember that an interview is two-way traffic. It is not just an opportunity for the interviewer to find out as much as he can about the candidate; it is also the opportunity for the candidate to find out as much as she can about your company, job, or project. The interviewers are selling the project so their demeanor is extremely important; they may be the only representatives of the company that your candidate will ever meet.

When it comes to lower levels of staff, a very good system is to conduct group interviews. Having five or six potential waiters in the interview room at the same time will speed up the interview process and will be enlightening. The interaction and behavioral dynamics among the group will tell you far more about each individual than you will be able to learn on a one-to-one basis. Remember, that in almost every job, there will be a high need to interact well with other employees or with guests. It is relatively easy to tell if an employee is technically competent from his track record; it is not so easy to tell if he will actually fit in.

Track records (resumes) are vitally important to study, particularly if you can find out about the standards and style of the places where the candidate has worked. The length of time that a candidate has stayed in each job is very telling, as, indeed is the reason that they left, a question you should always ask. Track records can, of course, be faked. That is why written and verbal references are important and why you should follow up on them and not just accept them at face value. Also, if you are dealing with large numbers of candidates in a foreign country, insist on a photograph of each one. It is not unusual, for example, to interview and accept Henry, who speaks perfect English, and then to find that he actually sends his cousin Herbert, who speaks none, to do the job.

Most important, however, is that during the interview process, look for and hire applicants who appear to have a positive attitude toward service and toward each other. In the end, if they are deficient in technical ability, you should be able to correct it; if they have a bad attitude, you may be stuck with it. Guests can be very tolerant of mistakes, especially at the opening of a new establishment and if the mistakes come with a big, warm, friendly, welcoming smile. This fact does not apply just to the guest contact jobs. All jobs in hotels are no more than one step removed from guest contact. If the dishwashers are always scowling, it will not be long before the waiters are too! Try to encourage an ambiance in which each job is seen to be as important as the next. Think of it this way: The captain of a jet liner might feel he is more important to the passengers, and his company, than the tractor driver that pushes out the plane, but if the tractor driver doesn't show up, or is always late, the captain is going nowhere.

Tip 34: Jump in the deep end.
The best way to learn.

Do not be afraid of opening the hotel at full tilt. Many hotel managers and companies conduct policies of "soft" openings with a view to weaning the new staff up to the desired standards of operation. I could not disagree more. I have never seen new personnel learn how to cope with pressure as quickly as when they absolutely have to do so. If a restaurant has a hundred seats, the quicker the staff learn how to cope with service of a hundred diners, the quicker they will learn to do so at the standards you, and the guests, require. Their learning curve will be steeper, but they will reach the required standard more quickly. One of the problems of offering the staff a "cushion" at the beginning is that they get used to a soft life, and then, some months after, when you remove the cushion, they find things too hard. In this regard, I am a great believer in the theory of throwing people in at the deep end; most people who can barely swim improve in a great hurry! Obviously, this theory can only work if the equipment and conditions are conducive to the staff being able to perform. It is no good expecting rookie waiters to cope with a full dining room if there is not enough cutlery to go around, just as it is no good expecting the swimmers to survive in the deep end if there are no steps to get out of the pool. That is why the logistics of getting the right operating equipment in place before the opening are so important, and why it is worthwhile putting a specialist in charge of this aspect exclusively.

The other benefit of opening full is that it creates a "buzz," and there is nothing more beneficial to a new enterprise than establishing the feeling that this is where the action is. The public facilities of hotels are designed to cope with a full house. If half of the hotel rooms are empty, it is not always easy to tell, until you look at the public areas. Naturally, if they have been sized right, and only half of the rooms are full, then only half of the public areas will be used, and these spaces might have the tendency to look cold and uninviting. Nobody wants to go into an empty restaurant, which is the reason a clever restaurant manager always sits her first guests where they are most visible. When the public areas of a hotel are too quiet, even in a brand-new place, the people who are there will start to wonder about its chances of success. If, on the other hand, it is difficult to get in, the word soon goes around, that this is a great place to visit.

Tip 35: Fish where the fish swim.
Pre-opening marketing.

You can't open full unless you have told the marketplace when the opening will be. This is yet another reason to fix a date and stick to it. Pre-opening marketing is, however, a tricky exercise and needs the special focus of people who are not bogged down with the detailed tasks of building, equipping, and staffing the place. It also needs a dedicated and, sometimes, substantial budget.

Ultimately, the best marketing of your project is through word of mouth, but initially you need to get enough mouths (and eyes) through the place for them to start talking. To do this, you must clearly identify your potential market and then concentrate your initial fishing on where the fish are, and where it is relatively easy to throw in a line or a net. Take aim at the deep rich veins; apply 80/20 thinking.

If you hope that a large portion of your business will come from tour operators, which, in turn, could be from twenty different countries, concentrate your efforts on a small handful of them. Select the countries in accordance with the season that you will be opening, the timing of their brochure production, the convenience of trade fairs, and so on. Be selective within the country itself. Rather than attempt to cover the full scope, concentrate on three or four big suppliers and offer them special opening deals that they will find hard to resist. Offer big support with cooperative advertising and promotional campaigns on a specifically targeted basis. Find out who their best retail suppliers are and mount campaigns, with their assistance, to hit these businesses hard with an awareness campaign.

For example, in opening the Coco Beach Hotel in Mauritius some years ago, out of the 8,000 retail travel agents in the UK, we targeted the top 800, whose customers where within easy reach of the airports with direct access to Mauritius (i.e., Heathrow and Manchester). We hired two teams of part-timers, students, and actors to "hit on" up to fifteen agencies per day with a colorful van full of coconuts, which were delivered to every desk clerk by a garishly dressed character brandishing a huge radio at full tilt. It did not take long for all booking agents in all of these retail offices to be aware that a hotel called the Coco Beach was about to open. Obviously this campaign was backed up with sales, price, and availability information, and the packages offered were put together with "never to be repeated" airfare deals, so that the coconut intrusion had a useful result. It took two teams exactly one month to visit (and disrupt) the 800 most productive high-street travel agents in England. Different campaigns were mounted in Germany, but little money was spent in the French, Italian, and Spanish markets, which were tackled later.

It is important to look for markets that can be switched on quickly and at the last moment. In most cases, this is a task too daunting to be tackled by the hotel alone. Do not be afraid to enter into deals with travel partners, but choose the right ones. For example, 80 percent of all arrivals into Dubai are through Emirates Airline. To enter into a marketing partnership initially with British Airways for this destination would seem to be akin to fishing in a poorly stocked pond. To build early occupancy at the Royal Mirage, our campaign allowed every person on Emirates who bought a first-class or business-class ticket to get their first night in the hotel free. This got them through the door in droves; needless to say, most stayed more than one night and many came back for future visits. It also helped Emirates sell higher-priced tickets.

It is also important to attract corporate customers because business travel is often enacted at the last moment. Fortunately, most businesspeople visiting their firm, or a client in an overseas city, rely on the local staff to make recommendations for accommodation. These recommendations do not always come from the local managing director; they may come from his secretary. Find out how things work, in this regard, right there at home base. Offer the decision makers the chance to participate in your opening activities, either as dummy-run guests or as part of the opening festivities, if any. Offer them very attractive opening deals. A few well-aimed bouquets in this direction can deliver business in great quantities and with great alacrity.

Tip 36: Kick-start the "buzz."
Throw a party.

In most cases, do not underestimate the importance of getting your new product known in the local neighborhood. Not only are many last-minute bookings delivered through local companies, but inbound tour operators also have a lot of leeway in switching reservations from an existing establishment to a new one. It is, therefore, important to mount a serious local public relations campaign; some of your best partners will be the local ones, and they are often the easiest and cheapest to reach. Many hoteliers are nervous about throwing opening parties and events, partly because they do not want to put the staff through stiff tests before they are ready. I feel strongly that it is important to "announce" your arrival on the local scene, to kick-start the "buzz."

When we opened the Palace of the Lost City, on the first three days we put on a spectacular Jean Michel Jarre sound-and-light show in the gardens of the hotel, utilizing the building as a backdrop. This event generated photographs in newspapers and magazines around the world (including the front page of the *New York Times*, some 7,000 miles away), and an enormous amount of international television coverage, not to mention the 36,000 locals who paid to see the show (and, of course, the resort!). Within one week of that event, we produced the Miss World Pageant on the site, which was televised in more than eighty countries (audience figures of over one billion) and immediately followed that with a Million Dollar Golf (winner takes all) tournament, involving twelve of the world's top twenty players, which was also widely screened on international television. It would have been quite hard for our target market not to know that a new hotel had been opened in "darkest" Africa.

When we opened the Royal Towers of Atlantis in the Bahamas, another mega-resort, we threw a two-day party to end all parties, to which we invited America's A celebrity list. Luckily for us, we had acceptances from Leonardo DiCaprio, Julia Roberts, Oprah Winfrey, Jimmy Buffett, Denzel Washington, Carmen Electra, Donald Trump, Ivana Trump, Monica Seles, Bob Arum, Quincy Jones, Harry Belafonte, Merv Griffin, Michael Jordon, Natalie Cole, Stevie Wonder, and Michael Jackson—the last three of whom got up on stage and gave an impromptu (and free!) performance to the invited guests. We then "set fire" to the new building with a cascade of fireworks, which blew the minds of this illustrious crowd, and beamed the pictures across North America. The hotel was almost full starting the next day.

These types of events do not happen by accident; they take a great deal of planning and a great public relations department. Naturally, not all new hotels can afford such extravagance and most do not need to. What is important is that, in your mind, if you are the person responsible for putting the new property on the map, *all* openings should be big events, and you should apply lateral thinking to create such events, no matter how limited the budget. It doesn't always take a lot of money to create a stir, but it does take a good idea.

5

Motivating the Operational Team

Tip 37: Avoid post-opening doldrums.
You're most vulnerable after you've scored.

Whether your hotel opening was a huge affair, or a mere blip, you had better not suffer too long from the hangover. Your task has now changed! For many months, and maybe years, you have been focused on one thing, and it has now been achieved. You will be tired, as will many of your team. But now is not the time to relax, for there is new work to be done. They often say that the most vulnerable time for a soccer team is just after it has scored a goal. How many times have you seen the opposition team pop one in to the back of the net, while its opponents are still celebrating? How many times have you seen a tennis player lose the next service game, having just won a set? There is a great tendency for this to happen in a new hotel. Often, the apparent lull after the storm of the opening develops into post-opening doldrums. This must not be allowed to happen, and it is your job as manager to make sure that it doesn't. Rather, think of the storm as a hurricane; you are now experiencing the "eye," knowing that it will soon pass and that you will be thrown into the back end of the storm in a hurry.

If you allow your staff to stay in the doldrums, the service they have trained so hard to achieve will suffer. They must focus on the bite-size goals that will lift the inevitably shaky opening service to higher and higher standards. Now it must be all hands on deck to deal with the guests. Sometimes, this new dynamic appears strange. For months, your team has been pulling together to achieve this clearly defined goal, almost without interference. Now there are strangers in the midst—hotel guests—and there can be a tendency to regard them as a nuisance rather than the reason for being there.

Tip 38: Punch your way out of it.
Clean up the snags.

If you think the builders have gone, then think again. As with all buildings, a snag list will develop, and it will doubtless be a long one. As cupboard doors are opened and closed, and showers turned on and off, things will go wrong. And these things will not only interrupt your efforts to give the best service, but they will need to be corrected in an orderly fashion. Just as you can be sure that something serious will go wrong during the construction period, you can also be sure that some niggling problems will go on and on after opening. I recall meeting the writer, Frank Muir, a guest at the Saint Geran Hotel, on day two after the opening.

"How are things going, Mr. Muir?" I chirpily inquired.

"Well, everything is fine—except the bed," he replied.

"Oh, what's wrong with the bed?" I asked.

"It's the legs. They've fallen oorf!"

He was right. Having tried to avoid the hefty import duties on beds imposed by the Government to protect the local industry, we had had them all manufactured in Mauritius. Unfortunately, the manufacturer had used, unbeknown to us, unseasoned wood—with the result that, one by one, all of the legs on all of the beds in the entire hotel collapsed within the first few weeks of opening. These events can be aggravating!

But many of the snags will be minor, and the tendency, therefore, is to live with them. Don't! You will only get one chance for the construction company or equipment suppliers to put them right. So, put a team on preparing a "punch" list of all the snags, however minor, and keep the construction people on site until every last one of them is fixed—even if it takes several months.

Tip 39: Focus in circles.
Don't run around in circles

Without clear and obvious goals in sight, it is now the manager's job to motivate the team by creating the goals. It will quickly become apparent, from observation and from guest comments, where the challenges lie, and these challenges must become the goals, both short and long term. There will, of course, be much "firefighting," but the manager must instill a sense of direction. As a manager, you will need to prioritize the problems and make solutions the goals. In managing any hotel, it is fairly easy to break down the tasks to be performed into three categories. These categories overlap and interlink, but most activities fall rather neatly into one or another of the three, which I encourage you to think of as three overlapping circles of focus. The three circles include:

Things to do with *guests*
Things to do with *staff*
Things to do with *finance and control*

As a manager, if you look at how your hotel is functioning in these three categories, you can start to departmentalize and come to grips with your problem areas. You can be sure, however, if things are going wrong in one of these areas, there will be a knock-on effect in the others. Initially, with the opening of the hotel, you would expect the problems to be in areas affecting guests (i.e., problems with the service). But, upon examination of these, you may discover that they are caused by other problems with employees. And upon examination of these, you may find that they, in turn, are caused by problems within the finance and control circle.

Tip 40: Get to the bottom of things.
Don't make assumptions.

For example, if the breakfast service appears to be the subject of much complaint, you may discover that the waiters are not getting to work on time to prepare for the service. After further analysis, you may discover that the early bus from the offsite staff accommodation has been canceled, and then you may find that the financial controller has inadvertently canceled it, because its load factor was not up to the quota he had set. In this example, you may have been tempted to assume that the waiters were not performing properly at breakfast (guest circle being affected by employee circle), when the real problem lies with the finance and control circle. The operations of any hotel can be analyzed in terms of these three circles (more of this in chapter 7), and it is normal that the manager's emphasis must change from circle to circle, as the needs of the organization change. Initially, after the opening of a hotel, it is highly likely that the emphasis needs to be on the guest circle. If we can't make the guests happy with our new product, we may not be in business long enough to worry about the rest!

Placing the emphasis on guest satisfaction as soon as the hotel is open is vital, and it may be that, to some extent, this has to be done at the expense of meeting goals in the finance and control circle. For example, when things do not go smoothly for a guest, for whatever reason, your ability to recover will be important. Guests will put up with service problems in a new operation to a very forgiving degree if they feel that someone cares. This "caring" may have to take place by offering a discount, or a bottle of champagne, or even a free stay. This will negatively affect the bottom line, but unless you can keep the customers happy, there will, eventually, be no bottom line to worry about.

Tip 41: Manage for the moment.
Being there: the golden rule.

The quickest way for you as manager and, indeed, for your department heads to get to the bottom of service (or any other) problems is by *being there*. If you realize that there are problems with the breakfast service, one morning on the site will show you where the problems are, without having to read about them in guest questionnaires long after the event and long after many other guests have suffered. In these crucial early days, there will be an enormous amount of paperwork, partly because a lot of it will be unfamiliar, and you will not yet have figured out what can be delegated and what is redundant. There will, therefore, be a great pressure on you to lock yourself in the office to clear the desk. You must resist this temptation at all costs, or you will soon find yourself with even more paperwork, reporting to you all the guest complaints and other things that have gone wrong.

To the greatest extent possible, get out of the office and into the areas where the action is. Your largest priority will be to get the service and standards right as quickly as possible. You can only do this by *being there*. But you can't, of course, be everywhere all the time. You can't divide yourself into little pieces. You must, therefore, be clever at choosing where you will be and when you will be there. This is not too hard to figure out. Look for the service pressure points and visit them. The first will be at breakfast. In a city hotel, breakfast is the most important meal of the day. It is often the only meal that your customers will actually take in your establishment. They are probably in a hurry. It can set either a pleasant or unpleasant tone for their business day. It can also be, if not properly set up, a complicated meal to serve, because of the huge variation in guests' desires and habits. This one wants a boiled egg "done" three minutes, this one wants it "done" four and a half minutes, this one wants hot milk, this one wants cold milk, this one wants skim milk. And most of them want it at the same time because they all have a plane to catch or a meeting to attend, and most people's business day starts roughly at the same time. This can be even more acute in a convention hotel, because most of the delegates will arrive late (and maybe hungover) for breakfast, but *all* of them need to finish the meal at the identical time.

Breakfast is often the last meal that hotel guests have before they check out; it may be, therefore, their last impression of your hotel, and last impressions are as important as first ones. Every piece of satisfaction building that has been done by your team during the preceding days can be wiped out with one unfortunate last impression. By being physically present at the peak of the breakfast service, either at the room service dispatch, or in the dining room, the manager can see where the bottlenecks and problems are. They will not require a brain surgeon to sort out. They will be problems due to design, equipment, supply, or personnel—all of which are solvable, once identified. The breakfast room is also a great place for the manager to meet his guests because it is one of the few places that they will almost all be present, albeit for a limited period.

The other location for last impressions, and a place that can come under severe pressure in the early morning, is the checkout or cashier's desk. It is also where your guest is presented with a chronological list (reminder and charge) of all the experiences from her stay. It is, however, the point at which you have the opportunity to say adieu or au revoir. It is a great place for the manager to be in the morning. It is a great place for the manager to hear what has gone right and what has gone wrong. It is a great place for the manager to intervene with recovery opportunities. It is a great place for the manager to show that he or she cares. And, it is a great place for the manager to demonstrate, as a role model, how the rest of the clerks should perform, and to support them when required.

Other pressure points can be identified, depending on the nature of the hotel. When a lecture in a convention concludes, there will be a rush for the bar (or the telephones or the toilets or the valet parking); when a big sporting event is being shown on the TV, there will be additional pressure on room service; in a resort, where the price includes breakfast and dinner, guests will be lining up for the dinner, and so on. Arrival times will be influenced by airline schedules or coach arrivals. And the mix of guests that you are hosting can change the ambiance of the hotel substantially. During school holidays, you may have to cope with hundreds of children who, unless properly entertained or catered for, will cause endless disruption and, ultimately, irritation to their parents. One happy child guest will invariably mean two happy parents!

If possible, having identified where the pressure will be, as manager, try to be there too. The benefits of this policy are enormous. First, you identify the problems in the guest circle, and, in many cases, you are the person with the key to the solutions. Second, your employees see that you are around, helping to solve *their* problems. Vice versa, you are there to evaluate how they, the staff, perform (employee circle). Third, you can also identify waste and bad control and pricing practices *before* they affect the profit and loss statement, not one or two months thereafter (finance and control circle). In addition, you will be seen as a role model, which is one of the most important motivators for your team. Establishing the right work ethic will go a long way to meeting the core values of your business.

Tip 42: Communicate: silver rule number one. Must know, should know, could know.

Being there—supporting and observing your troops—is the golden rule of motivation. There are, however, a few silver ones. Things often go wrong in organizations because employees are not always exactly sure what to do or are not given enough information to perform properly. We have all seen this in its most elementary form when a waiter who is questioned about the soup of the day must ask the chef. This circumstance reflects inadequate briefing and a lack of communication. Much of this lack of communication in a hotel is interdepartmental. For example, the arrivals list prepared by the reservations department is not distributed on time to the other departments that need it, or it does not contain all the information that they require to give good service. Or a banqueting salesperson fails to notify the banqueting manager that the client has asked for red roses on the tables, as opposed to simply "roses," resulting in a disappointed client and a frustrated banqueting manager.

Hotel organizational structures incorporate many built-in barriers to communication that need to be overcome. These barriers are commonplace between sales and operational departments, between kitchens and restaurants, between front desks and housekeeping, between room service and chambermaids, and so on. Salespeople are often criticized for promising things that either cannot be realistically delivered or can only be delivered if they are communicated clearly, correctly, and in good time, so that the operations people can prepare themselves. In the food and beverage area, often the junior member of the waiting staff places the order with the senior person in the kitchen. The needs of the housekeeper to clean the rooms in an orderly fashion may not fit in with the promises made by the front desk to the guest impatiently waiting for a room. The chambermaids may not feel it is their job to clear away room service trays. The list goes on and on.

A prime job of management is to ensure that communication channels are open and uncluttered. Everybody needs to have the task explained. Everybody needs to have the standard demonstrated. I always find it useful to break down information to be communicated into *must* know, *should* know, and *could* know categories. Clearly, an employee *must* know there are many, many things. A waiter must know where the plates are kept, which tables you are to serve, what each item on the menu means, and how to serve it in accordance with the standards of the house. There are also plenty of useful things that a waiter *should* know. For example, how many bookings there are for the restaurant, how full the hotel is, what the name of the hotel manager is, what time the swimming pool closes, when the hotel was built, where the salmon comes from, and so on. This knowledge is not essential to the waiter's performing the job, but it can help him prepare, enhance the way the job is done, and, most important, improve the experience of the guest.

Then there are the things that a waiter *could* know. These are not things that will help him perform the job technically, but they will make the waiter feel involved, motivated and proud to be part of a team. For example, he could know how much revenue the restaurant is budgeted to make, and how far ahead or behind the budget it is performing. He could know, even as a waiter, what occupancy the hotel is expected to achieve and whether this is being achieved or not. He could be taken on a tour of the presidential suite or even given the chance to experience staying in the hotel as a guest. If the hotel is part of a chain of properties, he could know how well the others are faring, and he could be offered favorable conditions for visiting them. None of these things will make him a better waiter, but they will make him feel more important and, therefore, motivated to play his part, as a waiter, with enthusiasm.

And remember, when you share information with others they have a tendency to share information with you. If a member of staff believes that you are communicating helpfully, chances are they will return the favor and let you know, from their important perspective, where things could be improved; things that you may never otherwise have known about.

With this in mind, it is important for a manager to reflect on how this waterfall of information is being communicated. It is clearly essential that you make sure that each supervisor is communicating the "must knows" to her subordinates, otherwise the standards of service required will never be achieved, but it is equally important that you make sure that all supervisors understand the benefits of passing on the "should" and "could knows," and that you give them the relevant information and tools to do so.

Tip 43: Lead with passion: silver rule number two. All aboard!

As manager, you must be passionate about your job. You must have a clear vision about what you hope to achieve and find ways to share this vision with everybody on your team. This vision is not necessarily exclusive to you. Ideally, it will be defined and refined from much discussion with your department heads and assistants. It must, however, be a vision that you personally buy into. It must be clarified by your insistence and determination. It must also be a vision that can actually mean something to those who are going to help you achieve it. Therefore, it must be definable and quantifiable in some form. It should also be crisp, pithy, and precise. Long-winded mission and vision statements are quickly forgotten, even by those who participate in inventing them. Maybe your vision is to be the best hotel in London. In this case, even though there will be many yardsticks to measure this vision, such as travel writers' polls, industry awards, the highest occupancy, the best rate, and so on, these things are, in fact, secondary. What is important is that "best" will have different meanings for your staff, and that it is a highly motivational word.

I once spent two full days in a think tank with about sixty of the most senior staff of Sun International in the Bahamas, trying to agree on a vision statement for the company to adopt. Our deliberations eventually produced four statements, which somehow incorporated our desire to have the best product, the best staff, the best value systems, and be the best place to work. The first statement was simply, "Blow away the customer!" It did not take very long for all other statements to be forgotten. "Blow away the customer," which was so easy to communicate and so pregnant with meaning, became the proud goal of every single caring member of our staff and contributed hugely to the success of the company. It was not long before hotel managers were adding these words to their business cards and letter heads, to their soccer team shirts, even to the back of staff toilet doors.

Having agreed where the business is going, it is important for you, as the manager to lead it in that direction with unflinching passion. You are the train driver, and the train, to use Professor Jim Collin's words, is "a passion train." All of your employees are passengers on this passion train. Everybody must understand where the train is going, and everybody must be enthusiastic about the journey.

Tip 44: Don't carry excess baggage: silver rule number three.
Only double-baggers welcome.

In all organizations, there are some members who do not have their hearts in the job, who do not share in the passion. In many cases, they will simply get off the train at the first convenient stop. Others, however, will remain as unwanted baggage. Your job, as manager, is firstly to find out why they lack enthusiasm (because often it may be due to the way their job is set up or to the fault of their supervisor) and to correct this situation. If, however, they continue not to share your passion for the journey, then you must throw them off, no matter how devastating the consequences might appear to be in the short term.

In one across-the-board training program that I conducted with about ten thousand staff, somebody likened these passionless passengers to "single baggers." I was intrigued by the description and asked for an explanation. My trainee responded by describing supermarket checkout personnel. She explained that there are two types of people in this position: those who cram your overweight groceries into one brown bag, with the result that it splits, and spews your purchases over the car park, and those who "double bag." From that moment, we worked hard to build a company staffed by double baggers. Even so, we ultimately decided that out of every hundred or so employees, there seem to be about twenty who can't be bothered with the second bag. As a manager, look for these people and get rid of them before they do damage.

In short, never be afraid to fire someone who is not up to or, worse, not interested in the job. You may be concerned about where to find a replacement, but someone will step up to the plate. The longer you carry the unwanted passenger, the more harm they will do to your business, and the more costly it will be to get rid of them. Throw them off the train! Someone once said that the two words that make America such a strong country are "you're fired!"

Some problems of ineffectiveness do not have to do with lack of passion, but with the inability to cope. This is sometimes due to the Peter Principle, which states that people in organizations are normally promoted beyond their capability. We've all seen this happen. A man does a good job as a restaurant manager and is promoted to become the food and beverage manager. There, he also does a good job, although maybe more in the area of service than control. Nevertheless, a vacancy occurs and he is promoted to hotel manager. In this role, however, he is not fully equipped to cope with the administrative duties. He tries hard to master these responsibilities but at the expense of what he is good at and, subsequently, performs poorly overall. Since he has previously been such a good and loyal employee, he is left in the job, underperforming. Imagine the same scenario across all of the hotels in the group. Sooner or later, every single establishment will be poorly run and the company will fail. You must not allow this to happen. If employees are not performing properly in a job, they must either be relocated to one that they can do (which will ultimately help them to sleep at night), or let go. I have had the miserable task of sacking many underperforming executives in my career. In most cases, although initially shocked and worried, they were in fact relieved. In many cases, they are still my friends.

Tip 45: Hire the best talent: silver rule number four.
Dealing with the difficult.

Some of the most talented people are the most difficult to work with. But the more talent you can have in your organization the better it will be, especially if you have stretching vision and passion. The hotel business is also part theater. It requires guests to be surprised; it requires them to be "blown away." Boring, untalented people won't do the trick for you. I encourage you to seek out talent; seek out prima donnas. If other organizations don't want them, that's great! You should find a home for them. They will be the people that will make a difference. If necessary, bend your organization chart to fit them in; don't bend them to fit into your organization.

There used to be an employee, called Harry, at the Beverly Hills Hotel in Durban. Every guest who had ever stayed there would remember Harry because he was such a memorable character. His job? Harry arranged the chairs around the pool. He never really fit into the organizational chart, but somehow or other, he made sure that every guest's need was met, not just in regard to the pool service but also in relation to restaurant reservations (either in or outside of the hotel), bets at the race track, special comforts in the room. You name it, and Harry would fix it.

Then there was Andre Damonte at the Carlton Tower. His job was head concierge. But far more guests knew Andre's name than that of the hotel manager. There was nothing (well, almost) that Andre would not do to please a guest. In theory Andre reported to the rooms division manager. In practice, Andre ran "Andre Damonte Limited," the concierge concession at the Carlton Tower. Did that matter? Of course not; the Carlton Tower guests were very satisfied, and they still paid top dollar for their rooms.

These people will never be easy to manage. They are not easy to contain. They need freedom to blossom. They do not take kindly to rules, and policies, and filling out forms. But if you can find a way of having others handle these aspects of the job for them, they will not only be grateful, but they will be free to perform. Do not worry that your organization will be overrun with them; these misfits are so rare that you will be extremely lucky if you can find enough to make a dent. They will, however, be hard work. Initially they will upset the rest of your crew, and you will need to spend plenty of time undoing the tangles they create. It will take patience to explain to everyone else the benefits of these misfits, and it will take a lot of patience placating the misfits after they have had their plans curbed or obstructed by someone else who objects to the expense, or the extravagance, or the lack of discipline. Eventually, when the results of the talent have blossomed, even the doubters will start to understand that the benefits are worth the pain.

Not all talented people, of course, are difficult. Some people have a very special talent of being able to fit in and cooperate with everybody else in the organization as well as do an excellent job and contribute immensely to its success. In hiring your immediate subordinates, do not be concerned that they all have their eyes on your job. Look for people who are capable of being promoted, even if, eventually, it is to your own position. During my career, I have run across many managers who specifically surround themselves with weak people who do not challenge them and, therefore, do not present a challenge. These managers feel secure in their own position. They are, however, completely misguided, because the results that they achieve, with their untalented team, are mediocre. Always look for assistants who are hungry for, and ultimately capable of, doing your job. This is the quickest way for you to be promoted.

Tip 46: Say thank you and well-done: silver rule number five.
Money isn't everything.

When there is a clear vision within a company, and reasonable and stretching goals have been agreed with employees, most people are self-motivated. Motivation comes from within and is fueled by achievement and a sense of personal pride and satisfaction in each employee achiever. However, achievement needs to be recognized, not only by the achiever, but also by the achiever's colleagues and bosses. When you ask a group of employees what has given them the most satisfaction in their jobs, they will always respond with words such as, "I was proud that I accomplished the task," or "I was proud that I broke the sales record," or "I was pleased that my department gained the highest standard award." They will often add, "I was so pleased that my boss recognized my achievement and said 'well done,'" or "I was so proud to be promoted as a result of my success." They almost never say, "I was so pleased to get a salary increase." Money, or more money, does not ensure employee satisfaction; if it does, such satisfaction is only temporary. Money is like food at its most basic level. You eat when you are hungry. You are not now really satisfied; you are just no longer hungry. One thing, however, is sure—within a few hours you will get hungry again. It's the same with pay. If you get an increase in year one, sure as I write these words, you will expect another one soon. Professor Frederick Herzberg called this phenomenon the hygiene/motivation theory. He likened pay rises to garbage collection (hence, hygiene). The garbage piles up every week. If the garbage collectors remove it on time you are not "satisfied," because you expect that to happen. If, however, they do not remove the garbage, you are really dissatisfied. The wrong paycheck for the work done is a dissatisfier. The right paycheck is expected.

This all goes to prove that time spent *recognizing* employees' achievements is some of the best time you will ever spend. Saying thank-you and well done, whether in front of their colleagues or privately, is vitally important. Caring for your employees, and demonstrating that you do, is vital. Make the attendance at funerals a priority, when they sadly occur. Make a fuss of people when they leave; don't let them feel they have been sucked dry. Obviously, you must remove the dissatisfiers or negative hygiene issues from the job, but outstanding performance needs to be heralded and then true job satisfaction will be ensured, and outstanding performance will be repeated.

Tip 47: Stand up and be counted: silver rule number six.
Take the rap!

Everybody makes mistakes, including you. Wherever you sit on the organizational ladder, if you have screwed up, be prepared to carry the can. Nothing will cause your employees and colleagues to distrust or dislike you more than not accepting the blame or responsibility for an error or misjudgment. Nothing that is, except, if you try to pass the blame to someone else.

Good leaders are people whom colleagues and employees can trust; they are people who fight for their workers; they are people who can be relied on for support in difficult times. Never allow that bond of trust to be broken. It can almost never be repaired.

Tip 48: Don't sit on the fence: silver rule number seven.
Neutrality is negative.

Don't sit on the fence. Don't always be neutral. Good leaders make decisions. Good leaders listen to advice and opinions, collect facts and data, and then have an opinion or make a decision. Employees don't mind working for people who, from time to time, make the wrong decisions; they hate working for those who never make any. At the same time, allow your employees to make mistakes. If you are running a business in which your employees are frightened of making a mistake, they will never take any decisions. They might avoid making any useful and profitable suggestions. They will also frustrate your guests.

These gold and silver rules for motivating employees are not the recipe for success; there are many more things that need to be considered and even each of these stated rules needs to be examined in more detail. However, if, as the leader and role model, you try to practice these rules, you will be well on the way to success and, to assist you in this, some of them are further developed in later chapters of this book.

6

Satisfying Your Guests

Tip 49: Get "into" your guests.
Traveling past the expectations.

Borrowing heavily from Abraham Maslow's *Hierarchy of Human Needs*, I have developed my own hierarchy of hotel guest needs. Maslow observed, many years ago, that human beings have a pyramid of needs and that those on the lower levels must be taken care of before the ones above. At the very basic level, humans need physical sustenance. Unless a human (or any other animal) can obtain sufficient food and drink, he or she will not survive. The next rung on the scale is security and safety. It is no good having a plentiful supply of sustenance if someone else can steal it from you or, worse, physically harm you in so doing. This search for security is also a search for adequate shelter. Human beings (and other animals) need a place to live, a place where they can both feel safe and obtain relief from cold or heat or rain or disease. These basic conditions must be met.

Having found a suitable place to shelter, human beings then make every attempt to turn it into a home with personal effects and homely comforts. Home, however, without someone to share it with, is not home at all, and so, for a mixture of motivations between loneliness, love, sex, companionship, and procreation, humans usually look for a partner. This probably motivates the need for a bigger home and better homely comforts. Humans generally, however, are gregarious, and certain social pressures start to emerge, such as a house as big as the Jones's, and soon the partners are seeking a better address, a bigger car, a flat-screen TV, and so on. Ultimately, none of these material comforts seem to satisfy them and they look for satisfaction from less tangible things. After all, how many Jaguars do you need in the garage, if nobody respects you, or if you feel as if your contribution to the world is useless?

The point, of course, is this. If you are starving, wet, and cold, your contribution to the world seems irrelevant and your sex life can take a backseat. One by one, the conditions on the pyramid of needs have to be met. Once they have been gratified in a sustainable way, they are no longer things that satisfy; they are things that are expected.

The needs of hotel guests can, to a large degree, be examined in the same manner. A traveler seeking hotel accommodation needs first to know that the hotel can provide shelter in a secure environment, as well as food and drink. If the hotel is situated in an unsafe area, or the bedroom doors don't lock, or the car park is badly lighted, the basic needs of the guest will not be met. It is no good having a friendly, welcoming staff, if you are starving or can't sleep in the place for fear of your life. Similarly, even if the hotel meets all of the basic requirements, indeed, even if it exceeds them with spectacular architecture and fantastic physical comforts, this will all be wasted, if the staff is unfriendly. To achieve perfection, as a hotelier, you must get the basics right first. Since the basics are commonly expected, however, they will not be enough to satisfy your guests. You must travel past the expectancies and deliver the unexpected, but this will be a waste of time if the basic requirements are not being met.

Tip 50: Go the extra mile.
Satisfaction is not what it seems.

I once conducted an experiment and asked a large number of hotel guests to tell me about their most dissatisfying hotel experiences. I then asked them to tell me about their most satisfying experiences. The two sets of answers were not opposites. For example, if a guest told me that he was extremely dissatisfied because the sheets were dirty, he did not then tell me how satisfied he was, in another hotel, because the sheets were clean. Conversely, if someone told me that the most satisfying experience was when a member of staff went out of their way to do something special for her, she did not tell me that she was dissatisfied because a member of staff did not do something special.

I, therefore, concluded that there is a list of basic requirements, which will cause dissatisfaction if not met. If, however, these requirements are fulfilled, they do not cause satisfaction—they merely remove dissatisfaction. Many hotel managers do not seem to understand this simple philosophy. When you try to explain to them that they are not delivering a satisfying guest experience, they take issue with you, on the basis that everything is running smoothly, and they do not have complaints. Not having complaints does not mean that you are satisfying your guests!

Do not be confused about food service. We often hear the phrase, "his hunger was satisfied," or words to that effect. I strongly maintain that if a guest is hungry, you will remove his hunger by feeding him. You can be sure, however, that a few hours later his hunger will return. A meal that really satisfies your guest will need to do more than merely relieve his hunger. You will have to give him exactly what he wants and likes, or, indeed, blow him away with fine cuisine. After all, you could take care of his hunger with bread and water!

It quickly becomes apparent that hotel guests become dissatisfied if the basics don't work. Guests expect a safe environment; they expect cleanliness; they expect hot water from the hot tap, and cold water from the cold one. When these things are in place, they do not write you letters of praise; they just are not *dissatisfied*. The "satisfiers," on the other hand, seem to revolve around the "software" of the industry rather than the "hardware"; that is, they involve the higher levels of Maslow's hierarchy and are concerned with social issues, such as companionship, love, and caring. Almost all respondents in my research, when relating incidents of high satisfaction, referred to an act of kindness, thoughtfulness, caring, or concern from a member of staff or management. They continuously mentioned staff who had gone the extra mile, staff who had foreseen or anticipated their needs and done something about them.

This should be music to the ears of hoteliers, because these "satisfiers" are mostly things that do not cost much. Few respondents stated that they were satisfied because the atrium lobby was two hundred feet high at a cost of many millions of dollars, especially after they had gotten used to it on repeat visits. Many, however, said they were dissatisfied with the length of the line to check out in the huge lobby!

It is, therefore, essential to understand this not-so-subtle difference. Spend the money, by all means, on creating a beautiful environment, but don't stop there, for this will be wasted money unless you create the "warmth" that guests can feel. Back in 1970, when we started Southern Sun Hotels, we had not read anything about vision statements or mission statements or core values. We did, however, have a logo that read, "You can feel the warmth," and it was not referring to the sunshine.

Tip 51: Listen to your guests.
Find time for feedback.

To find out exactly where your guests are on their hierarchy of needs, and to find out how well your hotel and your employees are performing in relation to the hierarchy, you need to *listen* to them. It will be hard to *hear* them if you are sitting in the office, unless, of course, they are so irate about something (or need something) that they insist on talking to you. Meeting your guests, as a hotel manager, is not rocket science, but it does take a good deal of planning and discipline to do it on a regular basis. Also, some managers are better at it than others.

To meet guests effectively, a manager needs to be around in guest areas at the busiest times. In a city or business hotel, two of these times will be during breakfast service and at the morning checkout rush. In many hotels, however, this time often coincides with the manager's urge to hold a daily "heads of department planning meeting," during which the problems of the previous day and the challenges of the upcoming one will be on the agenda, or the manager's urge to open his mail, or return phone calls that he has been thinking about on the way to work. Alternatively, if the hotel is part of a chain, there is every probability that one of the corporate (head office) executives will also be driving to work and decide to telephone the hotel manager with what (she thinks) is "urgent" business, just at the height of breakfast service and checkout. Obviously, if the hotel manager spends his time on the phone at this moment, or in a meeting, he will not get to listen to many guests.

I once conducted an interesting little survey of about a hundred city hotel managers about when they were on duty over a twenty-four-hour period. Most of them arrived at work between 7.30 and 8.30 A.M., whereupon they proceeded to their offices. Most of them left for home at about 7.00 P.M., having put in, of course, a far longer day than the average managerial or administrative person in another type of business. Most of their guests, however, left the hotel between 7.30 and 8.30 A.M., either to check out or to attend to their own daily business. A few returned for lunch, but most ate out. The majority of new arrivals tended to turn up in the late afternoon or early evening and those who had just been out for the day returned in the same period. Most hotel managers, therefore, were at home when most of their guests were at the hotel, and most hotel guests were out of the hotel when the manager was there. This, of course, demonstrated very clearly that every hotel manager should be very careful to spend as much time as possible in guest areas while he is on duty, to coincide with the periods when most guests are there.

Resort hotels, of course, are different because the pattern of behavior of the guests is not the same as in city hotels. Resort guests, however, can be much more demanding than those in city hotels, because the hotel is often the destination, rather than a place to sleep. In other words, the resort hotel is often the purpose of the visit rather than an incidental item. Resort guests often do not stray from the actual property. This gives them plenty of time to observe the comings and goings of the staff, and the levels of service that are meted out to other guests. Resort guests also tend to get to know each other, to talk to each other, to swap service stories, and so on. In short, resort guests have more time on their hands to observe the service standards and systems than the hotel manager does. A resort manager, who does not figure out how and when to talk to and listen to his guests, will be at a serious disadvantage.

Some hotel guests, whether they are in a city hotel or a resort, will seek out the manager to tell him exactly what they think about the hotel. Most won't. Most people do not care for confrontation or simply cannot be bothered to pass on their views, either good or bad. They are far more likely to do so with the housekeeper, desk clerk, or waiter, than with the manager, especially if they never get to see him. It is, therefore, incumbent upon the manager to approach the guest. Remember the silver rule about motivating your employees? Communicate. Well, the same is true with your guests. Communication is, naturally, a two-way thing. If you approach a guest, there is every chance that he or she will respond. Once confronted, you may find that it is like turning on the tap; you may get to hear about everything that is wrong (and sometimes right) about your hotel, as if you have just breached a dam.

Tip 52: Demonstrate you really care.
Sincerity and recovery.

The nature of your approach, however, must be sincere. We have all experienced the head waiter who sidles up to a table, before you have even taken a mouthful of food, to ask if everything is all right, and then moves on before you have answered, or doesn't hear your answer because he is on "remote." If you ask a question, you are wasting your time unless you ask it sincerely, and listen to the answer with interest.

There are other ways to obtain guest feedback, without actually speaking to the guests, but the benefit of listening to guests while they are still in your hotel is the immediacy. Obviously, if the guest's stay is going to continue, the current feedback gives the manager the chance to take corrective action and to make amends while the guest is still on the premises. Making amends, or "recovery" as many companies call it, is extremely important, because it demonstrates that you really care. Often, a minor complaint from a guest can be an opportunity to reverse the situation and create a customer for life. If you only get to hear about the complaint after the guest has left, you will still have a chance for recovery, but during the intervening period, who knows how many people the guest will have related her story to, including, maybe, her colleagues, her secretary, and her travel agent?

The other advantage for picking up on complaints about your hotel immediately is that corrective action can prevent the same problem affecting others. The most likely thing to happen, however, if you do not hear about the problems affecting a particular guest while in house, is that you will never hear about them. Other people might, but not you, and these problems will, therefore, persist to afflict other clients.

Tip 53: Don't rely on the summary.
Organizing feedback.

It is surprising just how much direct contact management can make with guests if a disciplined approach is taken. When I was an assistant manager at the Carlton Tower Hotel in the 1960s, the manager, George DeKornfeld, had an excellent system of forcing guest contact. Every morning George would take a clean copy of the day's arrival list and underline ten names. He would not leave the hotel that day until he had either personally met or spoken to "his" ten. However, George also sent a photocopy of his list to me and the other assistant manager, so that we could both underline ten different names. We, in turn, passed the list on to the housekeeper, the reception manager, and so on, right down to the chief engineer, and even, the accountant. Within an hour, George's list had multiplied by ten with a hundred names underlined; each "manager" did his or her utmost to make contact with "their" ten guests during the course of the day. The Carlton Tower had about three hundred rooms, with roughly one hundred arrivals per day. This meant that at some time or other, almost every guest was personally approached by a senior member of staff for feedback. Believe me, we knew exactly how we were performing on the guest hierarchy of needs.

Many hotel companies are not as disciplined as George DeKornfeld and depend on the guest questionnaire, which is routinely left in the rooms for volunteers to complete or is thrust at them as they leave. Whereas these questionnaires can provide useful data, the percentage that is completed is often very low, and the percentage of positive comments normally far exceeds the negative, often giving a rather too rosy picture. Furthermore, the review and compilation of these forms is often delegated to a clerk, or secretary, with only summaries reaching the hotel managers, or the company management. Also, if the guest questionnaires are addressed to, say, the chief operating officer of the hotel chain, but lodged at individual hotels, there is a huge tendency for the forms to be intercepted at the point of delivery, with bad news conveniently edited or "lost" before it reaches the addressee.

Tip 54: Wear the other boot.
Experience the guests' experience.

As well as gleaning as much data as you can from your guests, it is also important to put yourself into their shoes from time to time. A hotel manager should, as frequently as possible, experience what guests experience. He might start by simply phoning in to the place to see how long it takes the phone to be answered and how it is answered. Hotel managers should try making reservations at their own hotel, either for rooms or meals; they will often get quite a surprise!

It is also essential for a manager to stay frequently in his own hotel but not always in the same accommodation. It is amazing how often the manager, when required, or when convenient, to sleep in, chooses to stay in the best suite, or in his favorite suite. What he should do, of course, is to sample, bit by bit, all of the hotel accommodations, including the rooms at the back, the rooms next to the elevators or the corridor ice machines. Nothing will get the manager to understand what his guests have to go through quicker than by experiencing it for himself. He will soon find out that the instructions in the guest directory for working the phones are out of date, he will soon realize that you can't read which bottle is shampoo and which is bath gel, because the print is too small (most people don't shower with their spectacles on!), he will soon find out that the fax machine makes little beeps all night, or that the air-conditioning sounds like a tank coming through the window, or that the duvets are too heavy, or that "do not disturb" is not understood by the house-maids. He will also notice things that go unnoticed on regular room inspections; for example, the view under the washbasin when sitting on the toilet, or the position of the bedside lamps, while reading in bed, or that the bathroom lights are useless when trying to shave or apply makeup.

Even so, it is unlikely that the hotel manager will get a true reading of the standards of service being achieved, because word will spread quickly that he is "sleeping in," and he will be closely monitored. It is human nature that the staff will not want things to go wrong in this regard, and will modify their behavior to suit. To avoid this, it is sensible to employ "shoppers" or mystery guests (people who visit hotels in the guise of regular guests). They utilize all of the normal services but prepare detailed notes of their experiences, which are later compiled into information dossiers for feedback to management. Some of these "shopping" companies are extremely well organized and very experienced, giving the added benefit of comparison with competitors' standards.

A manager should also constantly examine his hotel from without. All too often, hotel managers do not go outside and look in. Remember, the hotel guest experience starts before the arrival at the reception desk. It may start with the directions that have been issued, either verbally or through fax or e-mail, as to how guests actually find the hotel. It may start with the street signage, or the actual driveway, or entrance, off the road, or a view of tattered flags. A guest's first impression is exceptionally important and often not very good, unless the manager has been outside to look in to see what the guest sees. The hotel front door is the equivalent of your own front door at home. It is, to some extent, a reflection of who lives behind it. A scruffy appearance, for whatever reason, will send a very clear signal of what to expect inside.

In many hotels the manager's office or other administrative functions are often located near the lobby and may be visible from the outside, particularly at the arrival point. If any of these offices are like normal offices, they will accumulate all sorts of filing cabinets and other office paraphernalia, the back of which will not look too good through the window, if the window is visible from the hotel entrance. Go outside and look in at night. If there is an office near the entrance, you can be sure that the lights emanating from it will be starkly different from those coming from the lobby or porte-cochère. These unpleasant views will be first impressions; they must, therefore, be blocked or filtered.

Make sure, too, that other entrances to the hotel, such as loading bays or luggage porter rooms, are properly screened. The last thing a guest wants to see, before reaching the front door of the hotel, is the garbage. In addition, as a developer, take care not to site the staff quarters, or indeed, the manager's house, en route to the hotel main entrance. I know of one beautiful hotel in the Seychelles where the arrival experience is completely spoiled by the location of management housing right at the entrance gate. Who wants to see the manager's family washing hanging on the line, or his kiddies' toys strewn all over the lawn?

Finally, as part of getting outside your own property, get to know your competition. Your guests have choices. It is essential for you, the manager, to understand what service and product your competitors are offering, and at what price. One way to do this is through anonymous telephone inquiries, or by examination of their Web sites, but the best way is to stay in your competitors' hotels or to send other trustees to do so for you. But remember, you are not there to have a ball. You are there to make very careful note of everything that is superior, or different, to your business. There is nothing wrong with copying a good idea.

7

Circles of Focus

Tip 55: *Look out for shifting sand.*
Where to place the emphasis.

In Chapter Six, I wrote about the three circles of a manager's focus, a simple analytical tool that I have found to be extremely useful. All activity within the business, with the possible exception of marketing, can be slotted into one or other of the circles, and can, therefore, be compartmentalized, dissected, analyzed, or grouped for the purpose of setting goals or solving problems. The three circles (groupings of focus) are:

1. Things that affect your staff (e.g., pay, morale, tidiness, attitude, pensions, staff transport, staff meals, locker rooms, training, etc.)

2. Things that affect your guests (e.g., standards of service, quality of food served, the greeting given at the front desk, the time it takes to answer a phone, the cleanliness of the room, the quality of the turndown service, etc.)

3. Things that affect your finances (e.g., the control at the delivery bay, the food portions, the cost of the meat, failing to charge the right price, waste, etc.)

The circles, however, are interlocking and overlapping. One circle cannot exist without the others and what happens in one will affect the others. For example, if one of your problems is the quality of staff meals, this matter sits firmly in the human resource circle. It does, however, overlap into the guests' service circle, because it may be affecting the staff's desire to give good service, or your ability to recruit enough staff to do so. It may also be affecting the finance and control circle, because it is keeping costs of operation down. Should you decide to take action and improve the staff meals, maybe by spending more on them, this will definitely have an effect in the finance circle, and, you hope, on the guest circle too, but it is primarily a matter related to staff.

If a hotel is well balanced in the way it is being managed, its good and bad qualities will be evenly distributed among all three circles. This, however, is not always the case, and it is reasonably easy for an outsider to walk into a hotel and determine quickly where management's emphasis has been. If the staff of the hotel is bright and cheerful, chances are management has been achieving its goals in the human resource circle. If, however, on examining the books, the food cost is found to be way out of line, or the amount of discounting from the rack room rates is exceptionally high, it becomes immediately apparent that the manager should focus more on performance objectives related to the finance and control circle.

The need for management focus will inevitably shift from time to time. If a new manager takes over a hotel and ascertains that the guest services are poor, he would be wise to place emphasis in the guest circle, possibly at the temporary expense of the others. He would need to identify the specific problems and solutions in regard to guest services and focus on them. The balance of his attention between the circles would therefore be initially lopsided. As, however, these service challenges are met and solved, the focus need will probably shift to the other two circles, to ensure all-round performance sustainability.

I have often been asked which of the circles is the most important. Their importance will vary according to the cycle that the business is going through. In a tough fiscal market, it may be necessary to be very frugal and hone in on waste and controls, even to the detriment in the short term of employee relations. However, on a long-term basis, if I were asked to allocate ten points across the three circles, in terms of their importance, I would do so as follows:

Guest circle	4 points
Staff circle	3 points
Finance circle	3 points

The importance of each focus circle does not necessarily mean that a manager must allocate his or her time in direct correlation to this distribution of points. Some very important actions take very little time, and some less important ones take more.

Tip 56: Work around the guests' clock.
Be smart with your time.

As we all know there are only twenty-four hours in each day, and most hotel managers seem to spend a great deal of them at work. Because of the nature of operating a business that needs to function on a twenty-four-hour basis, and in many cases, is even busier when most other businesses are closed, it is often necessary for hotel managers to spend more time on the job than the average manager in even another service business. Nevertheless, there are still not enough hours in the day for the hotel manager. As a result, it is vital for a hotel manager to choose her priorities well.

The nature of the hotel business can also be characterized as urgent. So many things that need to be done on a daily basis simply cannot be put off, because, if they are, it will be too late for any management action to have any effect. What a hotel sells is hugely perishable. Obviously, this is true of food. If food is bought in and prepared but not used reasonably quickly, it will be wasted. Everyone knows that. Rooms, however, are even more perishable. If a hotel room is not sold tonight, it can never ever be sold "tonight" again. You can't sell tonight's room tomorrow night. The opportunity to sell it has gone forever. Unlike most retailing, where the stock remains in the shop or showroom overnight (indeed, until it has been sold), a hotel room has a shelf life of exactly one day. This fact lends an urgency to the hotel business that is not unique (viz., cinemas and theaters), but does put it into a special group of businesses that need constant and urgent management attention.

The danger that lurks in this for management is a tendency for hotel managers to spend all day on issues that require immediate attention. So many items need to be checked, especially concerning guest service, that a manager may do nothing else but this. It is, therefore, vital for a hotel manager, to build a supervisory structure that can relieve her of the need to personally check every single detail of service before, and during, its occurrence. The supervision of guest service must be delegated, just as the supervision of the hotel accounts will be, but it must not be forgotten. A good hotel manager will selectively check the detail. Whereas a hotel housekeeper might perform fifty detailed room checks a day, the hotel manager may only perform, say, two. But these two will be selected at random, both in regard to time and location, and without prior notice to the housekeeper.

The supervisory structure of a hotel must be set up so that the hotel can function properly on a day-to-day basis without the intervention of the manager. Part of the manager's job is to test that the structure, and the supervisors operating it, are actually functioning well. If such checking becomes too routine, it will serve no purpose, because the staff will make special preparations; it must, therefore, be random and thorough. The only routine that a good hotel manager should settle into is not having a routine. A good hotel manager will pop up all over the place: in the middle of a quiet evening, when the rest of the supervisors and staff think that she has gone home, in the room service dispatch at the peak of the breakfast, on a Sunday afternoon when most of the staff think that she must be having a nap. In other words, the hotel manager must spend a lot of time "being there," but she need not advertise exactly when and where.

By ongoing analysis of her business, the manager should be able to adjust her focus and capitalize on the best use of her time. This analysis will be driven primarily by what she sees with her own eyes and hears with her own ears while "being there," whether the "there" is in the front or the back of the house, or even in a competitor's hotel. It will be supplemented, however, by the review of management information and data. A manager cannot be everywhere; a manager cannot count everything. As a result, it is incumbent upon the manager to obtain a constant and meaningful flow of information about the business. "Numbers" can speak volumes to a manager, if they are sensibly recorded and presented; "numbers" can also overwhelm even the best of managers. And, no matter how well presented the figures are, they are still a record of events, which by definition means that they refer to the past. In other words, the events that they relate to are history—and so may be your guests or your money.

What is all this telling us? A manager must spend time with her guests. A manager must spend time observing how the service is working for her guests. A manager must spend time with her staff. A manager must spend time observing how her staff and supervisors are performing. A manager must spend time reviewing the financial aspects of her business, both physically and on paper. A manager must set standards of service and behavior, select equipment and operating supplies, design collateral material, maintain the physical assets, set the prices, be there when the last reveler goes to bed and the first early departure rises, walk the dog, mow the lawn, play with her children, and stay sane. And all of this, before she figures out how to market the place! Is it possible to succeed in such a job? Only, if the manager is organized and properly supported.

Tip 57: Don't let meetings clash with your greetings.
Avoid guest hot spots.

The guest hot spots should, to a large degree, set the working timetable for the manager—but this will shift according to the type of business, the type of clientele, the day of the week, and so on. As previously stated, if a manager can position himself to be in areas of greatest guest activity, he will get more bang for his buck. Some time, however, will be needed to meet with his supervisors or assistants more formerly to review performance and plan. If these meetings are to be one-on-one, it is often a good idea to hold them on the supervisor's turf, rather than in the manager's office. Don't ask the chef to come to your office; go to his. You will still be able to have your meeting, but what you see and hear will be far more meaningful to you than what you learn within the walls of your office.

Group meetings are, of course, inevitable from time to time for effective interdepartmental communication and planning. They should be as brief and functional as possible, and held only if there is a reason. The reason for holding a meeting must never be the meeting itself. Group or departmental heads' meetings should always be held out of peak service times, and effective notes and recording of action steps are essential, especially to communicate with those who could not be present for service or other reasons. Such meetings are likely to fall into two categories: those that review and plan for the immediate short term (e.g., the day's events), and those that deal with longer-term issues. Be very careful to keep strict discipline concerning the length of time each meeting should take. People can get very comfortable sitting in a meeting, while their poor subordinates are sweating away in the kitchen or delivery dock. Always, as manager, maintain a "guest priority" rule. If a guest wants to see you or one of your colleagues while you are meeting, the answer is always yes. No guest should ever be told, following a request to speak to a manager, that he is "in a meeting."

Inevitably, you will need to spend time with your subordinates, not necessarily on matters related to the immediate content of the days work, but on their personal needs and performance, or other matters concerning their work or their staff, which can only be discussed in a quiet, nonstressful situation. These discussions may be best done in your office but always, if possible, outside of the hectic guest service periods.

Tip 58: Think things through.
Quiet planning time.

Between the greetings and the meetings, the manager must find some quiet time to plan and think. During this time, the manager must take stock of all she has seen and heard. She must also review all of the printed management information that has been assembled. Here, too, she must be selective. The figures and reports that have been compiled by others must be meaningful and useful. They must be broken down into bite-size, absorbable, chunks, so that the manager can relate them to the things she has just seen or heard about. For example, a figure depicting the value of the stock of food on hand might be quite meaningless, except as it relates to similar days in previous periods. A number that tells the manager how many days of food stocks are on hand may be much more telling, especially if she has just walked through the stores, but more of this in Chapter Eleven.

During this quiet thinking time, based upon the manager's analysis of the paperwork and the action, she should think through her business in terms of the three circles, and review her own contribution in this regard.

Tip 59: Do what does not come naturally.
Stretching.

As managers, we are role models. What we, as managers, do and say has an enormous effect on the behavior of our staff, and ultimately the service and the profits in our business. Unfortunately, like all humans, we have a built-in tendency to spend time on things that we like to do, and little time on things that we don't like to do. The result, of course, is that we get more and more practice, and become more and more at ease with, and, ultimately, better at the things we like to do, while becoming no better, nay, even worse, at the things we do little and badly.

The hotel business requires its managers to be proficient at a wide range of behavior, perhaps more so than any other business. Imagine yourself on a scale. At one end of the scale are things that require an immense amount of detailed focus, some of which may be quite mundane but necessary. Such requirements may involve production of accounts, stocktaking, pricing strategies, and so on. At the other end of the scale are extremely social requirements such as attending guest cocktail parties, making sales presentations or speeches, and so on. It is not abnormal for hotel managers to find that their natural abilities cover only a limited range on this scale. It is quite unusual to find a hotel manager who is completely comfortable with accounting principles and detail, as well as making speeches. Most of us have a predominant built-in strength somewhere on the scale, often with a bias toward one end or the other. Most of us continue to reinforce this predominant strength by continuing to spend most of our time doing things that we feel comfortable with, while avoiding the others. This behavior, of course, sends a very strong message to our staff. If the employees see that the manager spends all of his time poring over the accounts, while avoiding the guests, they will soon believe that the accounts are more important than the guests.

To become a better hotel manager, you must learn to stretch your abilities by doing fewer of the things that come naturally and more of those that don't. If you absolutely hate making speeches or presentations, force yourself to do so. The more you get used to doing things that you are not comfortable with, the better you will become at them, and the more comfortable you will eventually be. In planning your time as a manager, plan to do some of the things you do not like doing as a norm. Only by doing this will you eventually be able to operate a balanced hotel. When you have stretched your natural abilities to encompass the full range of behavior required, you will be a better manager.

Tip 60: Be prepared!
Understanding change.

No matter how great the hotel you are managing is, no matter how smooth your service is, no matter how efficient the business is, there will always be room for improvement. Perfection in any business is an elusive goal because things change—constantly. It is often said that the only certainty in life is change. Just as you think you have got on top of all the problems, resolved all of the difficulties, and achieved all of the goals, you will find that something changes, triggering new problems and requiring a new set of improvement goals.

This could be a change in personnel. If you have attracted the best people to work with you and have created an atmosphere where they can learn and prosper, chances are they will grow out of their jobs and start to need fresh challenges. You may have opportunities within the organization to provide these new challenges and you should always be alert to this need. If not, you will lose them, because somewhere a competitor can offer them more than you. Whether you are able to promote them or instead must lose them, the disruption that their departure might cause will need careful attention. Often personnel changes are completely outside your control. People get sick, or retire, or move away, if not sooner, certainly later.

The change may be a macro problem, something well beyond your ability to control. For example, a sudden switch in currency exchange rates can cause some of your key customer markets to dry up overnight. This is not theory; it is fact. Between 2002 and 2004, the value of the South African Rand versus the U.S. dollar rose by almost 80 percent. Room rates, which had been quoted to overseas tour operators some twelve months before, for inclusion in their travel brochures, suddenly rendered South Africa, which had previously been known as a good value destination, to be very expensive. Hotel occupancies fell. Likewise, the high value of the pound, versus the U.S. dollar in 2004, virtually caused the flow of Americans to London to stop. Major catastrophes can also have devastating effects on distant markets, completely beyond the control of individual hotel managers. The empty hotel lobbies across the world, after the tragic events of September 11, 2001, in New York, and the deserted resorts of the Indian Ocean after the Boxing Day tsunami in December 2004, bear testimony to this.

Change may also come in the form of competition. If you have been running an efficient and successful hotel, others will think they can do the same, and if economic wisdom prevails (often, even if it doesn't), you could soon find that you are facing stiff, and, by definition, newer competition. If the market you are operating in is very large, or if there are severe barriers to entry (such as limited supply of land), new competition may have a limited effect. But, if you operate, say, the only Holiday Inn on the Interstate Highway outside Akron, Ohio, and run at 80 percent occupancy, you can be rather certain that someone will soon build and open a competitive inn next door, and then you might both be running at 40 percent.

Tip 61: Go for your goals.
Setting improvement targets.

A good manager may not be able to predict change, but he will need to monitor it carefully and to take whatever action is necessary to protect, maintain, or even improve his business as a result. This will require setting goals, and specific targets within each goal, in order to assess progress and results. I recommend setting goals within the framework of the three focus circles. As manager, together with your assistants and associates, you must set goals for the business as a whole. Many of these can be broken down to form mini-goals, or departmental goals, for your department heads. All goals must be realistically attainable but must contain some "stretching." If they are too easy to achieve, they will be meaningless. They must also be measurable or quantifiable, and easily understandable. If they cannot be communicated clearly, they will not work, because almost all achievement goals will require input and effort from others. Each goal must have its "champion"; someone must take responsibility for achieving each goal, and they must all be set with time limits.

As a rule of thumb, it is useful for a hotel manager to work continuously on, say, between six and ten goals at a time. They will not necessarily all commence and/or finish at the same time. Some will take years to achieve, some only a few months. They will, therefore, need to be continuously reviewed, refreshed, achieved, added to, discarded, and replaced. They will act as a rolling scorecard.

Where possible, and when appropriate, a manager should spread the goals across the three focus circles. As manager, after review and analysis of the state of your business, and after full discussion with your departmental heads and other staff, pick the three or four most meaningful improvement opportunities from each of the staff, guest, and finance circles, and try to state in plain terms exactly what your goal is in each instance.

A typical set of hotel manager's goals might look something like the following:

Guests

1. To raise the level of facilities available for guests' in-hotel computer use to equal or exceed those of any direct competitor. Time for completion: 1 year.

2. To create conditions within the hotel where guests' pets are made as welcome as the guests themselves, with zero inconvenience to fellow guests. Time for completion: 6 months.

3. To improve room service delivery time to never more than twenty minutes (from order to delivery) for cooked items and six minutes for beverages. Time for completion: 4 months.

4. To establish a detailed and comprehensive guest history data bank, to enable the hotel to pleasantly surprise every returning guest in some manner. Time frame for completion: 9 months.

Staff

1. To ensure that every member of staff can speak a second language of their choice. Time for completion: 2 years.

2. To enable every member of staff (and partner) to spend at least two nights as guests in the hotel. Time for completion: 1 year.

3. To ensure that the salary and wage structure of the hotel is competitive within the industry, and that all remuneration bands, within the hotel, are appropriate. Time for completion: 6 months.

Finance

1. To improve the average daily room rate achieved by 2 percent more than the average increase in published rates. Time for completion: 1 year.

2. To decrease the average amount of food stocks on hand by one day's supply and the amount of beverage stock by two days' supply. Time for completion: 4 months

3. To produce the monthly profit and loss statement and balance sheet one day earlier. Time for completion: 6 months.

Each of these broad goals would need to be broken into a series of more detailed action steps with specific targets. For example, to achieve the first goal in the finance circle, one would need to examine in detail the makeup of the average rates actually charged and obtained, as opposed to the published price, to ascertain why and where there was slippage. One would have to examine and review the decision-making process in regard to room rates (i.e., who is entitled to authorize discounts?). One would have to review the mix between room sales and suite sales, the prices at the peaks and valleys, the authorization procedures for upgrades, and so on. Each of these items, and many more, would need to be analyzed, debated, challenged, and amended or reestablished, and this would have to be done in a disciplined, systematic manner within a specific timetable.

All goals, and more specific targets, would then be reviewed periodically for progress and, as goals are achieved, new ones would be added and reviewed in the same way. As manager, you will set your own goals, but much of the work of accomplishing them will be done through others, particularly your subordinates. You will also insist that your subordinates and departmental managers develop their own sets of rolling goals and objectives. To a large degree, their goals will mirror sections of your goals, but they will all include additional goals that are specific to their departments. Through this continuous process of analyzing the business and focusing on the weak spots, by setting and monitoring specific objectives, the business of improving the business will be accomplished.

Tip 62: Market by managing.
Happy guests come back.

By now some readers will be, rightly, challenging that not all of the work of hotel management falls within the three circles of guest, staff or finance. And this is true! The largest omission is marketing, which requires a substantial amount of focus in its own right. The reason that I have not included it within the three circles of a manager's focus is simply because I do not advocate anything that could cause a hotel manager to lose focus concerning his primary function. Marketing is essential, but the very best marketing that can take place is for all of the guests to return, or at least, want to return. Happy guests will, in theory, do your marketing for you, because they spread the good word. It follows that if the hotel management and staff are performing well, the level of guest satisfaction should be high, and most existing guests *will* want to come back. In a perfect world, therefore, a well-run hotel should not need the manager (or anyone else) to do any marketing; since all of the existing guests will be returning, there will be no need to find any new ones. There is also a danger that hotel managers will confuse marketing with taking overseas holidays. There is a great temptation for a hotel manager to combine his annual trip to Europe to attend a travel fair, such as ITB in Berlin, with a few weeks of calling on travel agents in nice places, that the manager or his wife would like to see.

This is not suggesting, of course, that the manager's visit to the offices of the source of a major supplier of business to his hotel is not a good thing. Nor am I suggesting that we live in such a perfect world that all of our happy hotel guests will return. Many would perhaps like to do so but are simply not able to or have no cause to return. The other reason, therefore, that I have, until now, left marketing out of the three circles is that it is one area of focus that is primarily conducted outside the walls of the hotel and, as such, can be "outsourced" beyond hotel management. It also requires such focus that it is worthy of its own chapter in this book.

Tip 63: Keep your eyes on the ball. Focus.

One reason for using the three-circle analysis is to encourage "focus" as well as to create a common language for such focus. Problems are never solved until they are focused on. Without proper focus—that is, with a superficial analysis, or "jumping to conclusions," or making assumptions—you might think that you have solved a problem, but it is generally not so. By focusing on a problem, I mean getting your mind around it completely, understanding it in detail, and feeling good in your "gut" that you really do understand it. You can only come to grips with a problem if you can focus on it properly. Otherwise, there is a great tendency for all of us to think we have solved a problem by applying a solution that worked for "yesterday's" problem.

Focusing on a problem takes time; it also needs an uncluttered (albeit temporarily) mind. If, for example, a hotel appears to be running very high costs in terms of "guest supplies," the problem will not be solved by sending out strongly worded memos to all staff, asking them to cut down on guest-supply waste. Waste may not be the cause of the problem, and such a memo might cause the staff to start cutting back in a manner that could reduce guest services. To solve this particular high-cost problem, you need to find the underlying cause. This will require an examination of all things that have actually been charged to "guest supplies", item by item. You might find the problem is right there. An accounts clerk might have had difficulty following the uniform system of accounts (or taken a shortcut) on a certain item, and wrongly allocated it. The high "guest-supplies" figure might not be "guest supplies" at all, but the cost of, say, vegetables.

Having established that all of the charge outs are correct, you would need to convert the cash figures in the accounts to the actual quantity of items. For example, it is quite difficult to identify waste of a particular item from the charged or allocated cost alone. A cash amount of, say, $400 for shampoo doesn't mean a great deal to me. If you tell me, however, that this figure represents forty bottles at $10 each, I can now relate the 40 bottles to the number of guests who have stayed in the hotel, and the cost of $10 per bottle as being something reasonable (or, in this case, unreasonable). Or, maybe, the figure of $400 means that we have used 400 bottles at $1 each. I will, of course, be familiar with the size of the bottles from "being there." Only by getting right back to the basic units used, and the unit price, can you actually test the reasonableness of the book entry, and the only way to do this is to insist on seeing the actual source documentation. On examination of the actual items, you might even find that the situation is worse than at first thought. For example, the bookkeeper, perhaps being protective of the purchaser (who may have actually bought 4,000 bottles), only expensed 400 during the month, and "hid" the rest in the stores under "operating equipment." You would now need to look in the store, and good luck if you can still find 3,600 bottles of shampoo there!

As an absolute certainty, if you dig deep enough into each of the items lurking under "guest supplies," you will eventually come across the reason the costs appear to be so high. It will either be a standards problem (an item specified as too expensive or an amount offered that is too generous), a purchasing problem (the wrong price being paid), a delivery problem, a storage problem, a wrong allocation problem, a stealth problem, or just basic lack of control due to sloppiness or untidy housekeeping. By focusing on the issue, you will discover what is wrong, and be able to initiate corrective measures.

To focus properly, you must clear your mind of other things and to break down issues to bite-size proportions. You must dig and dig until you reach the truth and discover the facts. Then, of course, you must focus on solutions and start testing their validity. Be warned, however, focusing the mind on a problem can be a very tiring exercise!

8

Marketing

Tip 64: *Manage your market.*
The importance of marketing.

Marketing hotels was a slow concept to catch on in Europe. After the World War II, few people were able to afford to stay in a hotel, unless it was of the seaside bed and breakfast variety, or the room above the pub for the traveling salesman. A few splendid grand dames of hotels existed in the major capitals or fun spots of the world, and the marketing of these seemed to be by word of mouth from one rich client to the next. I recall in the 1970s when the Savoy of London was sold to Sir Charles Forte, one of the outgoing directors, when asked about what marketing the Savoy had engaged in, replied, "Yes, someone goes to the market every day." He, of course, meant Covent Garden vegetable market, which happened to be just over the road.

In fact, hotels such as the Savoy carried out their marketing, very successfully at times, through one of today's marketing prongs—public relations. Before the hotel industry entered the mass market—that is, before the days of mass travel—hotel managers were required to be public relations men first, businessmen second. Most famous old hotels operated a type of dual management system. The so-called hotel manager was the front man, and the hotel controller was at the back. The controller, however, held the purse strings and often had equal power to the manager in terms of how the hotel was run. The controller naturally focused on the finance and control circle, without much overlap into the others except perhaps to curtail the hotel manager's expenditures. On the other hand, the hotel manager did not have to bother with the tiresome details of controlling the assets or maximizing the profits, which allowed him plenty of time to concentrate on looking after the hotel guests.

With the strong influence of American management philosophies in the second half of the twentieth century, the management structure of large hotels changed, and the controller found himself reporting to the manager, and the manager, as a result, had less time to spend with the guests. Before this, the manager was constantly engaged in public relations activities, both in his hotel and in his local community. Hotel managers were required to be "characters," people that guests would remember, or relate to, people that hotel guests would talk about to their friends, or people who could do special favors for their best customers. Nowadays, hotel managers will stage contrived events, such as the "Manager's Weekly Cocktail Party" to meet their guests. Previously, the hotel manager was always having cocktails!

Due to global economic expansion and the growth of domestic and international tourism, the number, and size, of hotels around the world expanded dramatically after Second World War, and their market extended way beyond a few privileged wealthy customers. As more people traveled, more hotels were required, and competition to satisfy this lucrative trade grew, increasing the choice available to travelers enormously. Although word of mouth and traditional public relations continued to play an important role in marketing hotels, other methods also had to be employed in order to bring to the attention of the marketplace the availability of the range of product. Brands were developed, and these helped to position the particular properties so that a prospective guest would know what to expect. Some hotels resisted being labeled or branded in order to stress their individuality and, by inference, the individual, personal service that they offered. Whether chain properties or independent, the hotels needed to gain the attention of the potential customers, and hotel marketing, therefore, spread from pure public relations to the broader reaches of advertising and sales.

Hotel marketing has now taken on such importance in hotel operations that it requires its own circle of focus. And the tasks to be undertaken within this circle are so time-consuming and complex that they simply cannot be undertaken by a hotel manager, without seriously eroding the time she would have to attend to the operation of the hotel itself. That is not to say the hotel manager should not be in charge of marketing her hotel, nor actively involved in key decisions or certain of the required activities, but hotel marketing requires very specific focus. Also, in respect of chain hotels, the benefits that can be achieved by marketing the chain as a group, rather than a group of independent entities, tend to take the role of marketing out of the realm of the individual hotel manager.

The hotel-marketing focus circle can also be broken down into three circles of focus: advertising, sales, and public relations. The engines that drive them are pricing and reservations (i.e., how much is charged for what and when, and how can clients actually find you to make a booking?). Technology has always played a big part in advertising and reservations, but recently there have been huge, and frequent, advances in this area as a result of the Internet, which has changed the face of hotel marketing and continues to do so at an ever-increasing pace. Any hotel or hotel chain that does not have an easy-to-access Web site, with user-friendly ways for an individual customer to make and pay for a reservation, will miss out on a large and ever-growing section of the market.

Tip 65: Price it right.
You can't sell it tomorrow.

Hotel marketing starts with pricing. I have previously described the perishability of a hotel room—if you don't sell it tonight, you can never sell it tonight. Because of this, it is vital to price your product so that it will sell, without, of course, doing anything, to devalue your brand. There is certainly a temptation to sell a room for whatever you can get, because sold, or unsold, your fixed costs are going to be the same; so, at a certain point, there is logic in pulling in any revenue you can, however small. You can't do this with a Rolls Royce, for instance, because there is little point in selling a "Roller" at below cost today, when you have a good chance to sell it at a profit tomorrow. However, like Rolls Royce, you have a reputation to sustain, and any deep discounting that you may be tempted to do during slow times will need to be carefully disguised or packaged so as not to damage your image, and, thereafter, hinder your efforts to get top rate in better times.

Pricing policies are extremely important to your enterprise. They are the cornerstones to your success. Pricing policies, and the rates resulting from them, should be understood, agreed, and signed off at the highest level in your organization. Reviewing and setting prices is not an exercise to be carried out amid the hustle of a normal day at the office; these are decisions that should be taken in a careful, quiet, and focused manner. To do this, you must stop the phones and concentrate. A few hours of intense concentration in this regard can pay huge dividends. Do not try to make these decisions "on the fly," and do not be pressured into making these decisions because a sales representative needs an answer now. Decisions taken in haste, in this regard, will be regretted at leisure.

There will be no more important decisions made in your business than what you actually charge, and how you collect what you charge. One of the underlying economic factors of price setting is this: If you can get, say, 10 percent more per night for each of your rooms without adversely affecting the level of occupancy, your bottom line will improve by 10 percent. If, however, you reduce your rate by, say, 10 percent, with the result that the occupancy increases by 10 percent, your bottom line will improve by something less than 10 percent, because you will have increased operational costs as a result of higher occupancies. Understanding and mastering this relationship between price and volume is one of the key skills of hotel management.

I know of one hotel chain that operates with only two prices. One price is for all individual customers, whether they are corporate or private, and the other is at a 10 percent discount for all groups of ten or more who stay in the same hotel at the same time. These two prices vary according to the season, and the days of the week, but no other special deals or arrangements can be made. The chain is a budget chain, City Lodge, and you could be the best friend of the managing director, but you would still not get a better rate than is published. This intransigent policy works for City Lodge partly because it is a budget chain and prices are already low. Its disadvantage is that it does not have the flexibility to engage in special promotions during low occupancy periods, but management believes that, if the rooms are priced correctly in the first place, there should be no need for such promotions, and that the cost of doing so would be greater than the incremental revenue gained.

This rigid policy will not be suitable for most higher-priced hotels, or for those operating in more complex markets, and, in these instances, a whole menu of prices will need to be determined. First, standard, or "rack" rates must be decided for each category of room, for each day of the year. These rates will be the basic rates from which all others will be discounted. They will be the rates that are published and publicly available to all comers. They will be the rates quoted to individuals who do not qualify for, or are not seeking, a discount. Rack rates should vary according to seasonal or weekly demand. Obviously, in times of high demand, rack rates should be as high as you believe the market will bear, but in periods of low demand, they should only be as high as competition will allow, since you will be operating in a buyers' market. Other rates will need to be set for group bookings, for corporate customers, for wholesale travel agents, and for Internet service providers. These will all, in some form or other, reflect a discount from the rack rates in varying degrees, depending on the overall revenue potential from each customer, on competitive prices, and on alternative sales possibilities.

In some instances, prices have to be set with long lead times because many of your clients, particularly the bulk buyers, will need to publish their sales material in brochures and the like many months before actual bookings will materialize. Lead times are getting shorter, as a result of the Internet, but a huge amount of business is still supplied to hotels, particularly resort hotels, through the traditional methods of a retailer (travel agent) utilizing printed brochures provided by a tour operator (wholesaler). In some countries, the wholesalers only print brochures for distribution to the retail trade on an annual basis, although these are often supplemented every six months with revised price lists. In other countries, wholesalers reprint brochures on a six-month basis, but the net result is that they need to have secured hotel rooms at fixed prices at least a year before the rooms are actually taken up and paid for. Although you, the hotelier, may have the opportunity to market special packages as addendums to the wholesalers' brochures and with their cooperation, it is likely that these will be "specials" offering a discount from previously published prices. A wholesaler is not going to put on a "special" that is more expensive than his original published price because he obviously would not make any sales. This situation is further complicated by wholesalers operating through the Internet who, although they have the ability to change prices at the very last moment, can seriously jeopardize your existing customers' arrangements.

The science of offering large blocks of rooms to wholesalers at prices set a year or more before delivery is complicated. Consideration must be given to your expected future operating costs, which means an understanding of the projected rate of inflation is required. If you are operating in country X, but marketing your rooms in country Y, you had also better have a good understanding of the potential strength or weakness of the respective currencies. Many resort hotels are located in Third World countries with high inflation and devaluing currencies. Often, your key operating costs, such as payroll, will be in one currency, but your revenues, primarily from overseas visitors, will be in another. You had better have a good understanding of the relationship between these two currencies before deciding whether to quote your rates in the local or the foreign currency. This can also be tricky because if, for example, you decide to quote overseas business in, say, U.S. dollars but offer a local currency (probably cheaper) rate to domestic business, you will find that local tour operators buy your rooms at the cheap rate and sell them to foreign wholesalers at the overseas rate. The end customer (the hotel guest who bought the package) will be buying at the higher price and the tour operators will be pocketing the difference.

You must also be careful to maintain the confidentiality of your rate structures. You may find that you are dealing with many different bulk buyers of your rooms, but some, of course, will be buying more than others. There will be pressure on you to sell rooms to the largest buyers at the cheapest rate, and it would not be unreasonable for the buyer to expect this. Be careful, however, that this buyer does not flagrantly pass on this discount to the public, because he will now be undercutting the price of his "package" relative to all of your other wholesale customers, who will, naturally, desist quite quickly from featuring your product. It is, of course, possible for a tour operator to disguise the price he is paying for a hotel room from his customers, and from other operators, by integrating it into a package with food, air, and land transport arrangements, but most competitors will be able to figure out his buying price, particularly if they look at the charges for extra nights, so confidentiality is not easy to maintain.

It is also important for a hotel manager to check that tour operators are not charging exorbitant markups, which are generating large profits in which the hotel does not participate. Some years ago, while visiting China as a consultant to assist the government in setting up their tourism industry, I was asked by the management of a huge hotel in Nanjing to conduct a one-day seminar on hotel marketing. About ten interested persons, all Chinese, attended my off-the-cuff seminar. I started by asking them to gather certain statistical information, such as occupancies and average rates, which they readily did. It quickly became apparent that, not surprisingly, the hotel, which had well over a thousand rooms, had two peak seasons, two shoulder seasons, and a low season, most of which were dictated by the weather (i.e., the hotel was full during nice weather in the spring and the fall, empty during the freezing winter, and half full during the hot and humid summer). These basic patterns were punctuated by local festivals, which affected the occupancy either positively or negatively according to the nature of the festival, and by external factors, such as school holidays in the overseas supplier markets. We then looked at where the business was coming from, and discovered that the largest single suppliers were a handful of tour operators from the U.S. West Coast . I called for a printout of the rates that these tour operators were charged by the hotel and, to my surprise, discovered that they were paying a flat rate per room year-round, irrespective of demand or occupancy level. We then located what copies we could find of the tour operators' brochures and, lo and behold, found that they, of course, were charging huge premiums for rooms during the nice weather, and more reasonable markups out of season.

On discovering this, and other similar facts, particularly relating to their exposure to only one market, we set about creating a new pricing policy for the hotel. This included all of the obvious things, such as charging higher rates for the rooms with the view, and differing rates for our newly named Platinum, Gold, and Silver seasons. Line by line we racked up our potential revenue gains on a flipchart and it was not long before, without improving the occupancy, by merely tinkering with the prices, we had potentially increased our revenues (at no extra cost to the business) by more than a million dollars. Satisfied that I had done a good day's work for the hotel, I now asked the assembled group to work out their implementation plan.

"Ah, there is a problem," one of the participants suddenly volunteered. "We cannot change prices."

"Why?" I retorted. "You have to change prices."

"Government no let us change prices," they continued, almost in chorus.

"Well, show the government our flipchart," I suggested.

They all looked a bit crestfallen. "Government only come set prices every other year. Not due here for over a year."

How things have changed in China!

Tip 66: Keep good records.
History helps.

It is important to review your rates on a regular basis. In regard to tour operator rates, the timetable for doing this will be dictated by the needs of each operator in each country. You are, however, at liberty to review and change rack and group rates, as often as you desire, subject to consideration of costs in printing and distributing these rates. Corporate rates may only be subject to change on an annual basis depending on your agreement with each customer. Before deciding on any change, you will need to analyze your cost structure and your need to bring in more revenue, as well as your recent occupancy performance, and the effect of your last round of increases. You will also need to take cognizance of your competitors' prices. This is relatively easy to achieve by making a few "false" reservation phone calls or Internet bookings, by examining their advertising, and by reviewing tour operator brochures, with particular focus on extra night charges.

You must also carefully maintain a rate history. The basis of your new rates will be changes to the existing ones. If you have proper records, it will be easy to identify the effects of previous decisions, and if you can do this in relation to a history of your competitors' rates, you will be able to take sensible, well-measured decisions for the future. It is also vital to monitor the differential between the average room rate that has actually been achieved and your rack rate. Say, for example, that your rack rate on a particular day is $100 for room type A, and $200 for room type B, and that you expect to sell roughly half of each type. Then, your potential average room rate sold for the day (or the period) ought to be $150. Due to all of the discounted rooms in the mix, you will find, however, that the average room rate actually achieved will be somewhat less than $150. If it turns out to be, say, $90 (i.e., a discount of $60 or 40 percent), but you know that your deepest discount is only 30 percent, then you will realize something is wrong. If, let us say, that the discount from rack is 20 percent as a norm, but all of a sudden, for the period under examination, has become 30 percent, then you need to find out why. You may be setting the rates very carefully, but some cavalier sales manager or desk clerk might be giving away the shop, without telling you, or putting all of the $100 customers in $200 rooms.

Tip 67: Keep your finger on the pulse.
Taking the temperature.

Room rate changes can generally be correlated to occupancy changes. If you charge more than the market can bear, or more than your competitors, unless you have such a unique product that everybody wants, your occupancy will fall. Similarly, if you are charging substantially less than your product can stand, or your competitors are charging, your occupancy is likely to rise—but you may be leaving money on the table. The dance between occupancy and rate is never-ending. The cause and effect can be quite dramatic and sudden and needs constant attention from management. It is a good management practice to monitor forward occupancies on a daily basis and to make ongoing comparisons with similar periods in the years before, hence the need for good record keeping. If, say, on April 1, your actual bookings for June are 10 percent or more less than last year on the same date, you may want to consider launching some special last-minute promotion.

Another temperature check to take regularly is the number of bookings taken on any particular day, irrespective of which dates they are for. If, for example, on a typical Monday, your reservation office takes a thousand reservations, or reservations for three thousand room nights (a different thing!), but for the last few Mondays has only taken eight hundred bookings, then the signs are that future business is soft. You might have excellent bookings for next month on a comparative basis with last year, but what about the months ahead?

In short, marketing management of a hotel or chain of hotels must constantly take the temperature of the business. The earlier one can detect softness in the forward bookings, the later one can take mitigating action, with the result that your competitors might be about to feel the pinch, but you will have foreseen the trouble. Mitigating action almost inevitably will mean a special promotion of one type or another. This may take the form of advertising a special deal, but this is a very public way of admitting that your business is soft and can lead to disenchantment from guests who have already booked at a higher price. If you are going to advertise a special deal, it is essential to apply conditions to it that will limit the problems of dilution of business you already have on your books. A better way to handle last-minute discounting is by aiming it at limited, ring-fenced markets, so that the general market (who might have already booked with you, or may be considering doing so in the future, at your normal rates) is not aware of it. For instance you might do a deal with AOL to target its customers on the Web, or with American Express for a marketing inclusion in a specific limited mailing piece, which gives Amex the right of saying that they have negotiated this extra benefit for their members only.

Tip 68: Make booking easy.
Reservations.

Special promotions will amount to nothing unless you can physically handle the reservations that are generated. Making reservations must be done in the most user-friendly manner possible, whether your customer is the travel agent, a secretary, or the end user. The first essential is that customers know where to make the booking, and the second is that the booking is handled efficiently. Obviously, the more direct bookings a hotel can take, the less commission it will need to pay, and the more rack-rate sales it will make. The cost, however, of advertising to the marketplace where, and how, a customer can make a booking at an individual hotel, is often not justifiable, and, therefore, hotels have either banded together to market conglomerates whose prime function is to take reservations (as well as to project a common image) or are part of a chain with enough critical mass to justify their own reservation infrastructure. The quality of group reservation services differs tremendously from company to company, and, like all businesses, is subject to the variability of the staff involved, their equipment, and, above all, their training. As a hotel manager operating within a larger reservations network, frequently monitor the network's standards by making reservations in your own hotel. In certain cases, telephone reservation agents have some discretion as to where they make the customers bookings; it is not a bad idea, therefore, for an individual manager, from time to time, to talk to, visit, or even send flowers to the reservationists. This is better than being anonymous.

The impact of computerization in reservations offices has been phenomenal. The potentially efficient way in which information can be instantly distributed to customers is now fantastic, *if* the actual systems are fast and user friendly. A bad system, such as one that gives you all the information, takes all of your requirements and personal and payment details, and then tells you that the hotel is full, can be a huge turnoff. Writers of computer software are not always typical hotel guests. As a manager, make sure that the system you are locked into is so user friendly that even you can use it. If not, fight like crazy, with whomever you must, to get it changed.

Tip 69: Understand your brand.
You'll get no surprises.

Branding is a complex subject. If a brand is working successfully, it will be sending a clear signal to the potential customer about the product. It will be saying, "This brand means that you can expect these standards and this value when you buy our product." Branding attempts to differentiate one product from other, maybe similar, products. A brand needs to be brought to the attention of the potential customers through promotion, signage, and advertising, and, therefore, the larger the scope, spread, and size of the branded entity, the more funds will be available to support the brand. Also, more branded outlets will increase customer flow-through, and good experiences in one outlet will promote future sales in other branded outlets. Success breeds success, but, likewise, a bad experience in one branded outlet will negatively affect all of the others, so failure can also breed more failure.

It seems to me that branding is particularly appropriate for hotels. Whereas I am not really sure why I need to choose between Exxon and BP, when filling up the gas tank, I do think it is helpful to have such guidance when it comes to more personal creature comforts, particularly those that affect the senses. In the absence of any internationally accepted grading system for hotels, and since it is so important to know that in a strange place you will not get poisoned, or strangled in bed, branding does seem to play a very useful function.

Tip 70: Learn from the past.
The history of hotel brands.

Hotel branding, at least in the form of multiunit branding, started in the last century in America, when Clemens Wilson created the Holiday Inn chain. Up until then America had been dotted with mom-and-pop motels and hotels. There was no national hotel grading system, so the traveling public did not know what to expect from a motel until they walked through the door. Holiday Inns changed all of that. The success of Holiday Inns was that the customer knew exactly what to expect—not luxury, but cleanliness, security, and a reasonable level of comfort and efficiency. One of the early Holiday Inn promotional tags was "you'll get no surprises at a Holiday Inn!" Other hotel entrepreneurs quickly followed, and soon there was a plethora of hotel chain brands across the country.

The battle to become the largest and, therefore, the chain with the most marketing dollars to sustain itself was on. But growing at a fierce pace was capital intensive, and the speed of growth of the rival chains was hampered by the limits to their financial resources. A solution was quickly found as the various brand owners allowed third parties to build and own properties to be operated under the brand name through franchise agreements, wherein the third-party owners paid the brand owners fees for the use of the brand and for marketing and reservation services. In the first instance the brand owners, to ensure maintenance of the brand standards, insisted on managing these third-party properties through management contracts. Holiday Inns and the others quickly realized that the returns from the sale of these services were far greater than the returns they could get from owning the bricks and mortar. Eventually, in the ongoing race to become the largest brand, third-party owners were allowed to manage their own properties under certain conditions.

At this point, things started to go wrong. Many brand owners were so hooked on the continuous cash flow from the fees that they went easy on enforcing the standards. The older properties in the systems were becoming obsolete and required either refurbishment cash or ejection from the system. Hotels managed by third parties and not kept up to the standard required by the brand were kept in the system because the fees to the parent company were attractive. However, as we all know, one bad egg in a box can spoil the rest, and this is exactly what began to happen. In some cases, instead of membership in a brand being an advantage to a diligent third-party owner, or even to those hotels still owned by the brand, it started to become a liability. The brand was only as good as its lowest common denominator.

In some instances, certain shrewd hotel marketing executives evaded the system entirely. They didn't own any hotels but set up marketing and reservation services for anyone with an independently owned property, provided the property masqueraded under the brand name of the reservations company. Companies, such as Best Western, started to round up a miscellaneous collection of hotel properties, labeled them all as Best Westerns and marketed them to the public as if they were managed by a common entity with universal standards. Some attempt was made, of course, to make sure that the member properties maintained certain standards, but these were, at best, halfhearted and were often not enforced if it meant the loss of lucrative fee flows.

Many hotel chain brands did not make these mistakes, or corrected them before the public at large had lost confidence in them, although it is probably fair to say that the brands that consistently deliver the standards that they promote are those that are still owned by the brand owners. Many brands also further strengthened their grasp on the market by expanding overseas. This expansion initially took place in Germany; after the World War II, there was a strong demand for hotel accommodation for American technocrats. Such personnel were wary of staying in a "foreign" hotel and Hilton International, which had been acquired by TWA, then one of the world's largest international airlines, seized on the need for Americans to be housed in a familiar "American" hotel, even if it was in the heart of Germany. A chain of Hiltons suddenly sprung up across Germany in Frankfurt, Munich, Stuttgart, Berlin, and even Mainz. Americans felt safe in these hotels; they could sleep on

American beds, drink American coffee, and be spoken to in American English. These hotels were very successful and were soon followed by Hiltons in London, Paris, and Madrid.

Not everybody coming to Europe from America could afford to stay in a Hilton, so cheaper brands, such as Holiday Inns and Ramada Inns, soon followed, and it was not long before Europe was dotted with hotels from an American culture.

The progress of the brands did not stop there. Soon the Far East, South America, Asia, and even Africa all boasted their particular variety of the American hotel brand, and all traded heavily on the idea that they were safe havens in strange places. Not all of the brands, of course, emanated from America or promoted American standards. Certain other brands started to spring up in other regions, such as Southern Sun and Sun International from South Africa, Kempinski from Germany, Trust House Forte from England, Mandarin from Hong Kong, and Meridien from France. Many of these chains played upon the fact that they were not American, as if that were an advantage.

In some international markets, the brands again began to prostitute themselves. It was difficult to control standards at long distance. Also, in many cases, the brands became overexposed and arguments broke out between different franchise holders. For example, one successful regional executive for Sheraton managed to convince several owners in Cairo to sign up for Sheraton services, with the result that a foreigner visiting Cairo had a large selection of Sheratons. Naturally, one Sheraton owner was suspicious of the next, when he found out that the Sheraton reservation service was sending twice as many customers to his neighbor's hotel.

The same problem occurred to a degree back in the United States. As trends and fashions changed, companies like Holiday Inns found that the product they had designed thirty years ago was now obsolete, and a new generation of hotels was beginning to erode the traditional business. As a result, these chains tried to get into the new markets by starting up other chains, such as Hampton Inns or Crowne Plazas. They attempted to differentiate them from the core Holiday Inns by pitching them at different price brackets, but, inevitably, the Holiday Inn franchisee was not amused to see his business being creamed off to a Crowne Plaza, which happened to be owned by his franchisor.

Tip 71: You can't beat the system.
Branding is here to stay.

Despite these difficulties, hotel brands are here to stay. It is also very hard to market an unbranded hotel, unless it has exceptional and unique qualities. Such hotels do exist, but they tend to be either at the very low end of the market, such as tiny bed and breakfast facilities, or at the very exclusive end, where the very fact that they are not part of a brand adds to their exclusivity. An example is the Sandy Lane in Barbados or the Savoy in London. Even so, these properties have found it necessary to be part of a global reservation service. Organizations such as Leading Hotels of the World or Leading Small Hotels of the World not only serve a useful purpose in operating reservation services at this end of the market but also help establish image for each property through their association in their sales material with other prestigious hostelries. In effect, therefore, the Sandy Lane is a brand in itself but takes insurance by being associated with another brand, for which it pays its dues.

If you are a hotel developer, you will probably find yourself having to select a franchisor that will suit you. If you are a manager, you will probably find yourself, at some time in your career, working for a branded hotel. If so, find out exactly what you can expect from the brand owners in the way of marketing support and what they, in turn, will expect from you. Often the squeaky wheel gets all of the oil, and this will apply to your dealings with the brand marketing department and reservations staff. In the case of central reservations, the actual reservationists can often be quite influential in directing business while talking to customers. If you can find a way of making sure that reservationists remember you or your property, then do so. Regular flowers, for example, to the central reservations office from the franchised hotel, that you happen to represent, might be a constant reminder that you are there. Or, continually bombarding the central marketing personnel with "crazy" promotional ideas that the brand owner will use his budget on but will specially feature your property might yield good results and make the sales executive look good. You will not be able to rely on the brand owners to fill your hotel. Their efforts will be far too broad to focus on your particular problems. At best, they will provide you with advertising that enhances the image of your property and makes sure that the standards of your sister properties are maintained, so that there are no rotten eggs to affect you. Unfortunately, there is no alternative but to directly focus on the task of filling your own hotel.

Tip 72: Practice public relations.
The importance of "ink."

One way to do this is through an ongoing and imaginative public relations campaign. The words *public relations* in the hotel industry have come to mean much more than just having good relationships with the public, be they the general public, the local community, or your customers. *Public relations* has come to mean any methods of promoting awareness of your property in the realms of the public without actually paying for advertising space. Public relations can, therefore, cover a huge array of activity designed to get "free" publicity and to make potential customers aware of the fact that you exist. As an individual hotel property, you will be unlikely to have the budget to take out paid advertising on a scale large enough to have any impact. If you can find ways of getting into print, or creating awareness of your product, without actually paying for ads, this will fall within the scope of what is now known as PR activity.

It is rare that a hotel can ever be a news event in itself, and it will, therefore, be difficult for any hotel to break into the news sections of newspapers or magazines. The exceptions to this rule are not often helpful, because a hotel is only likely to become a news item if something newsworthy has happened there. Often, such newsworthy events are ones that you would rather not be associated with, such as suicide bombings or mortar attacks and the like. You should, however, be alert to "good" news opportunities, such as a foreign dignitary or an international conference on your premises. Where there are press cameras, there are opportunities, and you should be alert to them. For example, if a visiting politician or newsworthy personality happens to hold a press conference on your premises, make sure that any pictures taken feature the name of your hotel, prominently displayed. In this regard, you must be a little canny. To a large degree, you will be in charge of the setup for the conference; that is, it will probably be your lectern they will use, or your stage, or whatever. It is your job to make sure that your signage will appear no matter the angle at which a picture is taken. And don't be too prissy about your signs. If you have a beautiful logo that you use on the soap and the letterheads, it will probably not be what is required as the backdrop to the photo shoot, because it will almost certainly be unreadable, when diminished in size to a picture on the front page of the newspaper. Take the key words that are important to you, such as "Hilton, London," and display them in the biggest print possible, irrespective of whether it conforms to your beautifully designed logo or not.

Because these opportunities are few, it is the responsibility of the person in charge of PR to manufacture photo and story opportunities. Fortunately, many journalists are lazy and like to be spoon-fed material, particularly writers for lifestyle sections of the paper or lifestyle magazines. Travel and lifestyle journalism is huge, and it is hungry to fill its pages. Fortunately, again, hotels fall neatly into lifestyle territory. The population at large is obsessed with travel, celebrities, food, and wine. You can provide fuel for stories in all of these categories. If you are diligent, you can get so many people writing about things that go on in your establishment that you will never need to advertise again. But don't expect the journalists to come to you; you will have to go to them.

Tip 73: Get into the glamour game.
The celebrity channel.

If you are fortunate enough to be marketing a hotel that might attract celebrities, local or international, you must find a way to use it to your advantage. Just as golfers like to play the courses they have witnessed the pros battling it out on, many people like to stay in hotels that have been promoted by famous people, even if such promotion was inadvertent. La Mamounia Hotel in Marrakech is a great example. Winston Churchill used this hotel as a rest and relaxation station during times of stress. Many of his paintings were conceived in its gardens. The penthouse suite is, naturally, called The Winston Churchill Suite; the whole hotel has been marketed on the back of this famous guest for many years.

Another example of using celebrity power to promote a hotel is the now defunct, Landdrost Hotel in Johannesburg. The Landdrost was being built as a block of apartments when, as part of a more complex deal, it was taken over by Southern Sun and turned into a hotel. Unfortunately, the hotel was not in the best part of town (subsequently proven as the area deteriorated further, and the hotel eventually became a police hostel). It faced serious competition from Western International's Carlton Hotel, which was located in the best part of downtown, adjacent to covered shopping malls, cinemas, and so on. Southern Sun had to put the Landdrost on the map. First, the hotel was decorated exquisitely, with many striking and glamorous suites. Second, the hotel included a state-of-the-art cabaret restaurant/night club, modeled on London's hot Annabelles; in fact, it was even called Annabelles. The hotel was certainly the sort of place showbiz people would like to stay, but, unfortunately, it was at the wrong address.

Notwithstanding, management went out of its way to attract every famous person that ever set foot in Johannesburg, film star, politician, sports personality, whatever. If management got wind, normally through a network of public relations agencies or through contacts with the press or the entertainment world, that a celebrity was coming to town, the offer went out for him or her to be housed in one or other of the glamorous suites for next to nothing. As a result, there was a constant flow of famous people through the doors, and, of course, a constant flow of pictures in the newspapers as well as TV, press, and radio interviews, all coordinated by the hotel's public relations staff.

The Landdrost also got involved in many promotional events that were going on in the city. For example, when a local tennis promoter was arranging a celebrity/pro charity tennis tournament, she found herself short on celebrities. Through the contacts of the Landdrost management, she was able to attract Richard Burton, Elizabeth Taylor, Ringo Starr, and Peter Lawford to play in the tournament and, naturally, they all stayed at the Landdrost and spent every evening in Annabelles. As a huge side benefit, management persuaded Richard and Liz to visit a new hotel that Southern Sun was opening in Botswana, the Chobe Game Lodge. Richard and Liz were so enchanted with the Lodge (and with each other) that they decided to get married there. The resultant publicity was so enormous that the Chobe Game Lodge, for a while, was a household name across the world.

There are, of course, many hotels that, by their very nature, will not be able to generate publicity through visiting guests or celebrities, and PR, as described here, would be impossible. However, this should not stop management from having a PR mindset. Whether it is letting the local cops know that there is always a free cup of hot coffee available at your place, helping the mayor with his election banners, providing free meeting rooms for the Round Table, or sponsoring the local school cricket team, do things that will make local people think of you when it comes to housing their overflow relatives at weddings and funerals.

Tip 74: Think laterally.
Staging events.

Dreaming up and staging events is a major role for the PR department. From the birth of Sun City, South Africa, the dreaming was constant, and several major events evolved that required a professional PR infrastructure, involving press rooms with facilities for wiring stories and photos all over the world, TV satellite links to ensure uplift of television pictures, and all of the necessary outside broadcast facilities.

For example, one of the first promotional events to be created there, the Million Dollar Golf Tournament, is still broadcast around the world every year, twenty years after its inception. The format was simple. The professional golf tours, both American and European, finish at the end of November and start again in January. This left a window during December when no tournaments took place and gave the golfers a chance to have a holiday with their families. Sun City management took advantage of this window with an offer that even the richest golfers in the world found hard to turn down. The top ten players in the world rankings were invited to play four rounds of golf for a winner-takes-all prize of one million dollars (over the years this prize has increased to two million dollars), which at the time was, by far, the largest first prize for a golf tournament. There were to be no second or third prizes. Each player had a ten-to-one chance of earning a quick million. But, in addition, Sun City made sure that it invited the wives and the children to South Africa for the holiday of a lifetime. The format worked, and even during the darkest days of apartheid, the top golfers in the world continued to look forward to participation in the event, which was beamed to countries across the world with plenty of Sun City signage prominently displayed. Just as important, was the event's effect on the local market. For four days, every day, more than twelve thousand people streamed to Sun City to watch the household names of golf, and a good few finished up in the casino (golfers included). Also Sun City management was able to take forty of its very best customers and invite them to play in a pro/am tournament on the day before the event proper. Imagine what "brownie points" you get by arranging for your best customers to play a round of golf with Jack Nicklaus, or Tiger Woods, or Ernie Els.

Other PR opportunities may be more mundane but also take a lot of organization. Many involve creating articles for travel or lifestyle magazines. It is not difficult to dream up events involving food and beverage or music, sport and entertainment. Just think laterally. In New Orleans I was once involved with a problem hotel. The hotel was obsolete and needed a complete renovation. The hotel was situated next to the Superdome and, therefore, "sport" was an obvious theme to focus on. We came up with the idea of renaming the hotel, which was called the Warwick, to the "Players," and decided that, rather than allocate numbers to every room, we would name them after famous sports persons and would decorate each room with personal paraphernalia to be supplied by the players. We drew up a list of several hundred famous sports personalities from a worldwide range of sports. The deal was that, if they supplied us with, say, ten personal items, such as a photo of themselves as a baby, an old school report, a personal letter, perhaps a trophy, we would use these to decorate "their" room, on the understanding that, if ever they were in New Orleans, they would be able to use their room for free. To our surprise the world's most famous sports personalities started sending us not only their photos, but also their cricket bats, their racing helmets, the "caps" for representing their countries, their trophies, and much, much more. Soon we had a whole storeroom crammed full of the stuff. They must have all cleared out their attics!

In addition, we contacted the world's premier sports painter, Leroy Neimann, and we persuaded him to let us call the restaurant Neimann's and to decorate it with his famous paintings in exchange for 2 percent of the restaurant revenues. Leroy was delighted to oblige. We also arranged with *Sports Illustrated* magazine to nominate the Players Hotel New Year's Honors every year, through which, in conjunction with the magazine, we would award ten new sports persons rooms at the hotel.

Alas, when everything was ready to proceed with the renovations, the owners of the hotel went bankrupt, and the whole process had to be halted. Sadly, we returned all of the gear to the players, who reluctantly put it back in their attics. Nevertheless, it was still a good idea, and illustrative of what a piece of lateral thinking can achieve.

Tip 75: Choose creative administration.
The advertising agency.

Another weapon in your marketing armory will be paid advertising. This will fall into one of two categories, either image advertising, or selling a specific deal or offer. Either can be achieved through direct paid advertisements or through paid advertorials (i.e., articles that are placed to promote your product but do not appear to be direct advertising).

For most independent hotels, paid advertising in national or international media, whether press or TV, is far too expensive. Advertising in local media and on the local radio stations may be an option; if so, the same disciplines need to be followed that would be for an advertising campaign by a major international hotel chain.

Advertising is probably essential to promote a chain of branded hotels, and the marketing executives of the chain will decide how, what, and where to get the best bang for the buck, because plenty of bucks will be required. Advertising is a special art, and hoteliers would be wise to recognize that it is best to use specialists. These experts proliferate as advertising agencies, so the first task in preparing an advertising campaign and budget is to select the right agency. An advertising agency does not normally mean extra cost. Because of the agency's ability to buy advertising space in bulk for a full range of clients, the reduced advertising tariffs available to the agency fund the costs of working with the agency. In addition, an agency is likely to be able to get "control" over key advertising positions in the media as a result of its bulk buying. Getting the right spot in a paper or magazine is very important. Agencies have studied how people read newspapers, including the people in your particular market, with the result that they know the best pages to advertise on, the best position on the page, the best papers to advertise in (for your particular market), and the best days of the week to spend your money.

Choosing an agency is not easy. Agencies are very good at selling themselves. Agencies put their best salesperson onto this job. This is often the boss, or the founder, of the agency but may not be the person who is going to carry out your work. Just as you did when you selected the interior design firm, you will need to know who is actually going to handle your account, what they have done before, how long they have been around, and so on. There are two main types of people in advertising agencies: the administrators and the creators. You will definitely need an administrator on your team because much of the work involves the detail of negotiating for advertising space, creating advertising schedules, controlling the billing, and so on. However, your ideal account manager will be an administrator with a creative flair, an administrator who understands creativity, an administrator who is respected by the creative people in the agency, and one who can conjure out of them their most creative work for your account.

As in all selection processes, look at the track record of the agency. They will be quick to show you their success stories; you must also ask them to show you their failures. Carefully examine the type of work they have been doing and balance that against the type of work you will need. If, for example, they specialize in advertising for manufacturing companies or distribution companies, they may be the wrong crowd for you. It may be better to select an agency that understands service industries, but don't insist on it, because great creativity can transfer quite easily from one area to another. Large agencies have certain advantages. They have more clout in buying space; they have more backup if the account executive leaves, or gets sick, or goes on vacation; but they also have many accounts to handle. In a smaller agency, your account might become the most important, the one they least wish to lose, the one on which they all focus. These are the elements that you will have to weigh carefully.

Having selected your agency, you must give the people time to understand how you and your business work. Let them come into the business, let them immerse themselves in it, let them understand your core values, let them experience what you have to offer, let them sense it. But then, make sure they understand that you are the boss, that you make the decisions. If they are very creative, they will come up with loads of zany ideas, most of which will be impractical. You—not the agency—must decide what you are going to do with your advertising budget.

Tip 76: Promote the photo.
Creating the image.

Image advertising will be the most subjective. Everyone will have an opinion. No one will know who was right, even after you selected an approach and went to print. Image advertising must be designed to do just what it implies, create an image for a brand. This must be very carefully thought through, but the task is somewhat easier than for many other products that require image building. Take perfume, for example; how do you advertise a smell? You can, of course, attach mini sachets to magazine pages, but this is pretty tacky. So what do you do? You show pictures of beautiful people, just like the people you wished you looked like, waving around bottles of perfume in various states of ecstasy. And you make the shape of your bottle more exotic than everyone else's. With hotels, at least you have some physical product that you can photograph and display. If you wish to convey an image that your chain is a place where you can get some serious business done, then you might photograph your no-nonsense room, with its handy, computer friendly, desk. If you wish to convey the message that your hotel is one where you can get away from it all, you might use a picture of your perfect and isolated beach.

Much of image advertising comes down to great photography. Once again, you will find yourself in the selection game. Getting the right photographer for your "mood" shot is not easy and is not cheap. Use the agency to help you select the best in the world for your particular need. It should have access to data on the sort of photographers who will be suitable. Use the agency to negotiate with the selected person, and, most important, use the agency to direct the actual photo shoot. In this day of point-and-shoot digital cameras, it may surprise you to know that a great photographer will probably only produce one or two actual usable shots per day. The detailed planning necessary for each shot will stagger you. Deciding the dressing of the room, what exactly goes on the plate, the mood lighting, the outfits of the models—all need to be planned in infinite detail. Then, there are certain moments in the day when natural light is magic, but these moments are fleeting and must be planned.

Also, remember, great photographers will take great pictures, but they may not be the pictures that you want for commercial reasons. For example, the artist in the photographer might see a great photo opportunity in storm clouds over the beach. You, the hotelier, will not want the lasting image of your beach to be a shot of a storm. After all, on your beach the sun always shines, the wind never blows, and it never rains!

The photo shoot must be planned carefully for other practical reasons. You may decide that you want people in your pictures to create the impression of a buzz, or you may decide you want pristine shots with no human in sight. You can be sure that, unless the shoot is properly coordinated, you will find unwanted hotel guests in your pictures, or if you want them, they will be wearing or doing the wrong things. Plenty of photographic time and expense will be wasted unless the whole affair is properly organized, and all of this will be magnified if you are shooting for TV.

When you get the finished product, choose very carefully which ones you will use in print. Make sure that the pictures tell the story that supports the image you are trying to portray, but make sure that they are also practical to use. Study them carefully; blow them up to the size they will appear in the paper or, worse, on a billboard; figure how they will work together on a page; see how they can complement each other. The photos will be one thing, but how they are cropped and how they are utilized to best effect is another. Then, when you have selected the pictures you are going to use, make sure that all photos you have paid for, whether used on this occasion or not, are now properly categorized and filed. These pictures are extremely valuable. They must be regarded as currency. Unfortunately, what often happens is that they are not treated as valuable items; they are left lying around, or lent out and never retrieved. Over time, one of the most valuable assets a hotel marketing department can build up is a photo stock, which, because of its value should be kept under lock and key and administered by someone as strict as your local librarian. Good pictures can be used repeatedly for future advertising campaigns, for supplying tour operators, for incentive group organizers to put in their blurb, or for your own future company brochures. Most hotel companies squander their stock of pictures unashamedly.

Tip 77: Dare to deal.
Two for the price of one.

Advertising for specific deals or promotions presents different challenges. Normally the pictures required will take on less importance, and the detail of the offer will take on more. Hence, the need to ensure that the detail is clear, concise, and thoroughly understandable. There must also be a call for action. If the reader decides that he or she wishes to take up your offer of a "great spring break" or a "fantastic family holiday" or "two rooms for the price of one" or whatever, she had better be able to clearly identify how she does so. The instructions for making reservations, or for asking questions, must be crystal clear. Then, as marketing executive, make sure that whoever has been designated to field the phone calls or the e-mail inquiries is aware that the offer has been made and knows every intricate detail, so he can take bookings or answer questions. This will mean that before the details of the offer are finalized, they should be thrashed out with the people at the sharp end of the business (i.e., the head of reservations or front desks, or the relevant hotel managers). Then, sufficient personnel should be available to take the surge of bookings or inquiries that you anticipate will come from the publication of the offer. If, for example, you decide to advertise your wares in the Sunday papers, it is no good asking people to call your reservationists if they are closed on Sundays, or if they are operating with their normal scaled-down Sunday crew. Reservations personnel must be scheduled to coincide with the advertising exposure. This may sound elementary, but it often does not happen.

Keep careful records of the volume of phone calls received after the publication of each advertisement. These records should be analyzed in terms of actual bookings taken and actual queries. If the ad generates lots of interest but few actual bookings, something is wrong with what is being offered. If the volume of calls, immediately after the advertisement appears, is little more than generated in the normal course of business, then something is wrong with the advertisement. It would not be the first time that the call to action in the newspaper carried the wrong phone number, and, if this were to happen, someone is to blame—and that someone is probably you, because you didn't do what all hoteliers must do, check the detail. Insist on seeing the proofs of all advertisements that carry special offers or deals, and check the details: the dates, the prices, the phone numbers, and so on. The only thing worse than paying for an advertisement that is incorrect is paying for it twice!

You must also be very careful that your special-deal advertising does not clash with any ongoing image advertising. If your brand is being positioned in the minds of the public as a very exclusive product, then it could be very harmful to that image if ads start to appear that focus exclusively on price, like a hardware store or a supermarket. Having a sale in the luxury goods business is always tricky. Harrods, in London, has done a great job in this regard; it has managed to elevate its annual sale to an event. Many companies get rid of their unsold rooms, or seats, by having third-party "bucket shops" do the discounted sales, thereby distancing the brand from the offer. Other companies own their own travel wholesalers, who then market the rooms, in disguise, so to speak, but this can upset other travel company suppliers, who become suspicious that the brand is giving special deals to its own travel wholesaler and, thereby, creating unfair competition. If you decide to advertise directly and to take direct bookings, it is not a bad idea to select some of your best suppliers, and allow them to feature as part of the call to action in the advertisement. In other words, it is not smart to cut out the travel trade that supplies you with ongoing business. Going it alone can be equivalent to biting the hand that feeds you.

Deciding exactly where to place advertisements is also a challenge. You will be faced with a very large choice. You must decide which type of media to use. Should it be newspapers (national or local), magazines, billboards, radio, or television? The latter is very expensive and can really be considered only by branded chains. Not only is production expensive, so is the actual purchase of the slots. Nevertheless, television, as we all know, is a very powerful medium. Radio should not be overlooked, because in most countries it is much more regionalized than TV and is, therefore, cheaper and more flexible. Also, many radio stations will deal with hotel companies on a barter basis, by swapping air time for hotel room nights or meals, which they then use as prizes on radio programs. Whatever medium you choose, you will then have to decide where you will actually use it. Here the principle is quite straightforward: "fish where the fish are swimming!" Study your market and decide where are the best volumes of business possible. Make sure that you have the infrastructure in the target market either by operating with partners in travel or directly, to handle the business to be generated by the advertisement.

You will never have enough cash in your budget to advertise everywhere, so you will be forced to prioritize and to limit spending to your biggest markets, and, even then, to the fullest "ponds" in those markets, bearing in mind access to your property, or properties, from such markets. Obviously, if your hotels are in Kenya, but there are no direct flights from Oslo to Kenya, you would not be wise to spend much of your advertising budget in Norway. Similarly, if you believe that there is good potential for business from the United States, the country is so big and the media is so regionalized that you cannot possibly spread your budget across the whole place. You should, therefore, decide which is the fullest "pond," as well as from which "pond" is it easiest and cheapest to get to your destination. Much of this research will lead you to conclude that you cannot go it alone with your marketing program; you will need to coordinate your efforts with airlines, national tourist boards, local travel wholesalers, or others.

Tip 78: Pick promotional partners.
Working with others.

The hotel industry is encircled by a host of enterprises, which feed off and service it. These include outbound tour operators or wholesalers, retail travel agencies, Internet booking services, inbound tour operators, incentive travel organizers, national tourist boards, airlines, travel clubs, and so on. There is a tendency for hoteliers to regard these groups as enemies, rather than as partners. That is because, in various forms, they extract a slice of the hotelier's room rate in commission or discount. Used properly, these organizations are an invaluable and helpful tool for filling your rooms. Unless your product is so exceptional, so unique, and in such demand that you don't need these partners, you would be unwise to attempt to cut them out because they will return the favor. Some of these organizations have vast tentacles wrapped around the traveling public and, in many instances, large marketing budgets, which you can tap into, to steer that public through your doors, rather than someone else's.

Try to conceive marketing or advertising campaigns in each location with a partner in travel. A joint promotion to the airline's frequent flyer members will be far more cost-effective than going it alone. Embark on an advertising campaign that shares the cost with a travel company on the basis that the bookings are taken through that company, rather than directly by you. A special offer to all American Express cardholders might gain you access to the right market, as indeed could be an offer in the BMW owners' magazine, or the like. Be prepared to share the cost and the reward.

Take great care, as a hotelier, to respect your partners in travel. There is a great temptation for a hotel manager to approach a regular guest whose booking is normally made through an agency with a suggestion that a better rate might be made available if the agency commission could be avoided. This is a short-sighted policy. Rather than fight the people who feed off you, use them.

Tip 79: Support your sales team.
Selling at the sharp end.

No matter how good your image building has been through public relations and advertising, and no matter how many direct bookings you can generate from your Web site, you will still need a direct sales team. In most hotels, except for highly specialized or niche operators, your sources of business will be the following: corporate, convention, incentive or other groups, tour operators and travel wholesalers, direct, via the Internet or your company reservation office, third-party reservation systems, or walk-ins. Some of these markets will need to be serviced by your own employees, who can negotiate prices and sort out the required detailed arrangements. Depending on the size and scope of your enterprise, you will need to have sales personnel to develop one-on-one relationships with, at minimum, your potential suppliers in the corporate, group, and travel markets.

Despite the rapid growth of direct bookings through the Internet, the public at large is still wedded to the system of booking vacations through retail travel agencies. Travel agencies are the shop windows for travel wholesalers' products. Some travel agencies are owned by travel wholesalers and some by air charter operators; these travel wholesalers produce multiple-destination brochures, which are racked in the retail travel agencies. Travel agency staff is trained to be familiar with the product on offer in the brochures, as well as to effect bookings. In some countries, there is a multitude of travel wholesalers, whereas in others, a few operate in an almost monopolistic manner. Some wholesalers specialize in certain areas of the world, some specialize in certain types of holiday, some appeal to the "tailor-made" market, and some to the mass-market budget traveler. If you have decided to offer your wares in a particular market or country, it is essential that you understand the structure in that area of the travel trade. You must know who the key players are in the area that interests you, and then you must understand how they can be serviced. This will undoubtedly mean that you will need to provide a salesperson to interact with the wholesalers whom you need.

This salesperson will need to understand the critical path for the production of the wholesalers' brochures. She will need to negotiate the largest exposure possible for the product in the brochures as well as the prices that you are willing to extend to each wholesaler, bearing in mind that they will be in competition with each other. This will be a tricky process, because each supplier will try to obtain from you a price lower than his competitor, either so he can keep more of the markup for his own company, or so he can offer a lower package price than his competitors. Your salesperson will have to tread the delicate path of giving everyone what they want without giving away the shop, or upsetting any of the suppliers.

On a practical level, your salesperson will also have to provide the wholesaler with the relevant information about your product and suitable pictures at the right time, and to use her best endeavors to influence or control how your product is displayed. This task can be onerous because most of his wholesale customers will be attempting to publish their brochures at roughly the same time. Much of the salesperson's success will be based upon her relationship with her counterpart in each wholesale company. This relationship can only prosper if the salesperson is able to deliver what is required by the wholesaler in a helpful and timely manner. If your salesperson is able to develop a reputation within the industry of being trustworthy, helpful, and efficient, you will certainly reap the benefits of extra exposure through your travel partners. It will be up to you, if you are the salesperson's boss, to organize yourself in such a way, as to be able to supply that salesperson with the information and material that she requires on time. Remember, it is not your salesperson pushing you for decisions; it is your customer.

The travel sales staff will also have to plan to attend trade shows, but here they will need to be selective and organized. The biggest travel trade show in the world is the annual ITB in Germany, followed by other important shows in England, the United States, France, Dubai, the Far East, and elsewhere. Specialist travel shows, for conventions and groups, are held at other times. Typically, at these shows, countries, travel companies, airlines, and hotel groups take the exhibition stands. In the larger shows, the exhibition halls are divided into such groupings, and the countries are often divided by continent. Here sellers are given the opportunity to display their wares and to attend meetings to discuss rates, problems, or opportunities. You will have to decide in which hall you wish to exhibit, if at all. If you represent a group of hotels, you may wish to be in the branded-hotel hall, but then you may miss out on opportunities for your individual hotels to participate in stands from the countries where the hotels are located. Often buyers of rooms concentrate on geographic areas and, therefore, if you have a hotel in Africa in your group you might be well advised to have some representation in the African arena.

There is normally such a frenzy of activity at trade shows that it is not all productive. Much time can be spent on socializing, rather than furthering the business, so sales representatives have to approach these shows in an organized fashion by pre-scheduling meetings with buyers before the show commences. Generally, trade shows offer a fantastic opportunity to present wares to the travel trade at large, because they will offer one of the few chances to address the entire industry in the same location. It is usually desirable for a hotel company to invite its customers to an after-show evening function, but be aware, that you will be competing, in terms of time slots for this, with all of your competitors. In this case, the most well liked and respected salespeople will draw the largest acceptances for such events.

Other salespeople in your organization or from your hotel will be needed to service your corporate customers. Many organizations arrange group travel for companies. In the United Kingdom alone, about fifty companies do nothing else but arrange incentive travel groups for British companies. Many organizations, such as professional groups like doctors or dentists, hold annual conventions. Decisions as to the location of these events are sometimes made two to three years ahead of time. If you want your locations to be in the running to host these events, you had better have your salesperson on hand with all of the relevant information, when the location decision is made. On an even larger scale, the venue for events, such as the Olympic Games or the Soccer World Cup, is decided upon through competitive processes at least eight years ahead of time. The hotel company that is most supportive of its country's bidding committee will probably reap the biggest benefits in the event of a successful bid. All of these leads can produce massive business. If you want to participate in such business, make sure that your salesperson is there, when required, being as helpful, informative, and cooperative as possible. These group bookings are important because they give you an opportunity to establish a base level of business on your books well in advance, normally at good rates, which enables you to plan your strategy for how to attract shorter lead-time business and to establish the likely gaps in occupancy that will need to be filled by special promotions.

A good salesperson is hard to come by. He or she will need to have that special blend of likeability and attention to detail. The latter quality is extremely important because the salesperson will be protecting your average rate achieved and making sure that all of the details required by the customer are correctly recorded and passed on to the operations teams. A salesperson who promises things that are not possible will not survive long, nor will the salesperson who forgets to pass on to hotel or banqueting management the many specifics required by the customer. The likeability of the salesperson will have to extend to his operational colleagues, as well as to his customers. One of the barriers to organizational efficiency is between operations and sales. It is normal for hotel operations staff to complain that the sales staff has sold something that is difficult to achieve and, often, at the wrong price. For this reason, the salesperson must be particularly empathetic in regard to the capabilities and nature of the operations staff, while coaxing them into ever better performance. A salesperson who is disliked by the operations team may find his projects sabotaged.

9

Training

Tip 80: Create confidence in others.
The power of self-belief.

I cannot emphasize enough the importance of training. Many readers of this book will be currently undergoing some form of training, either formal training in university or college, less formally in a company training scheme, or informally in the school of life. Many of your future employees, however, will not have been so fortunate to have received any training and what they have picked up in the school of life will perhaps be from a very different life to that of their customers. There is often a huge gap between the experiences we have had and the experiences our customers are used to, and expect to receive from us. In plain words, it is difficult to know what caviar tastes like if you have never had any, but your chances of so doing are quite slim unless you are rich or lucky.

What good training does, apart from teaching people technical skills, is to give them the confidence to perform such skills in front of others. Most of the so-called skills used in the hotel business, with the exception perhaps of cooking, are not skills at all; they are job content. Although it is difficult to call making a bed a skill, nevertheless, there is a right way and a wrong way to do it. In short, good training is the art of teaching someone how to do something to the standard you require and with the *confidence* that will ensure that it is successfully implemented *in a manner that will please customers and colleagues alike.*

To know how to train, we must understand how people learn. If you want someone to learn a skill or maneuver that they have not tried before, you must first establish an environment that is conducive to learning. Most trainees will feel nervous about trying out any new task, and a threatening, or maybe even competitive, environment will make them even more so. Nervousness makes it more difficult to listen well. Nervousness is sort of an interference to hearing. It is a bit like listening to a radio station that is slightly off-station. Instead of concentrating on what he is being shown a trainee will concentrate on not being nervous. This, of course, is wasted energy. Imagine how this nervousness is multiplied in situations, in which the trainee who is from a Third World environment tries to learn how to give service to a First World client. For this reason, a good trainer must first put her trainees at ease. The trainer must be empathetic to the background of the trainee and must assure the trainee that this is not a race to see who can do something first. We all learn at different speed. Some of us move slower than others but are more successful in the end. Remember the hare and the tortoise?

To teach something, you must first demonstrate it or explain it. You must do this clearly and often enough for your trainee to understand it. If it is a complex task, you must break it down into bite-size chunks and demonstrate each chunk at a time. You must then ask your students to copy what you have shown them. If they get it right, give them positive feedback; if they get it wrong, you must also give positive feedback about the pieces they got right, as well as further demonstration of the pieces they got wrong. Give them time to practice, using each practice session as an opportunity to fine-tune their performance. Continue giving positive reinforcement until your trainees' confidence levels are high. This process is a continuous loop of demonstration, practice, feedback, demonstration, more practice, more feedback, until perfection.

Learning and performing in a classroom, however, is, at best, crude preparation for performing the same thing under the pressure of service, or in front of a customer. Unless your trainees are supported through the early stages of "live performances," there is a real chance that confidence will evaporate and they will fail in the task. If the trainees are supported long enough for them to gain confidence, their aptitude for getting the task done even better will quickly grow. The most crucial part of the training process is, therefore, supervision on the job. I once wasted six months of hotel school training, which I had arranged for about a hundred rural Africans, during which they had been taught the menu cycle of a new hotel, because under the pressure of the opening, I was not able to supply enough support to them. As a result, everything they had learned and were able to do in the classroom disappeared as difficult guests shattered their confidence in the first two days of operations. Many never regained their composure and simply went back to the bush.

It is also useful to let your customers know that your trainees are just that, trainees. It is amazing how much more helpful most customers are to a struggling server wearing a badge marked "trainee" than to a struggling server the customer believes is incompetent.

Tip 81: Understand and respect each other. Cultural differences.

Hotel keeping is a global industry. We, therefore, have to deal with many different cultures. There will be many times when the culture of our employees is vastly different from the culture of our guests. Not only must we address this issue to ensure that we are giving our guests what they culturally require, but we must also address it to ensure that we understand the culture from which our employees have been drawn. What is regarded as polite behavior in some cultures is regarded as rudeness in others. For example, the Japanese have been taught to avert their eyes when shaking hands; in the West, this behavior would be considered shifty or rude. I was once in China, looking at some potential development opportunities. My wife, Diana, had come along for the ride. According to the local custom, I traveled in one car with the chief honcho from the Chinese host company, and Diana traveled in a following car with a Chinese junior executive and a driver. I discovered at the end of a four-day trip that every time Diana and her host got into the car they had gone through a performance as to who was going to sit in the front. Diana, thinking it was polite to offer the front seat to her host, was constantly disturbed to find out that he didn't seem to like this but reluctantly accepted. It turned out that, whereas Diana thought she was doing him a favor (more leg room, better view etc.), he thought he was being demoted to the staff seat.

In Africa, there is a saying, "The white man has the watch, but the black man has the time." Most white people translate this into meaning that they get things done on time and that blacks are always late. The black African translates this into meaning that the white man is always in a hurry, whereas he has the time to do things comfortably and properly. Unfortunately, in Africa, we often find ourselves, in the hotel industry, trying to provide service to white men with watches with black servers who are far less concerned with the time. The resultant harassment that a member of staff can receive from the guest is often inexplicable to the African and saps his confidence.

It is easy to confuse a laidback style with inefficiency. Because certain cultures take what appears to be a happy-go-lucky approach to life does not mean that they are stupid or lazy—far from it. A few years ago, I was conducting a training session with a group of twelve junior supervisors in Africa. They were a mixed-race group, consisting of eight black Africans (mostly from different tribal backgrounds), two white Africans, and two Asian (Indian) Africans. I decided to use an exercise designed to illustrate some important features of good communication. The exercise involved splitting the group into two teams and, within each team, allocating roles to every "player." In each group, each player drew straws to determine his or her role. One role was as chairman of the company, one as managing director, two as supervisors, and two as workers. Each team was asked to sit at a table with cardboard barriers separating the players; each barrier had a slot through which they could pass written notes. The chairman was given a task to perform, which he or she had to achieve solely by passing notes to the managing director. In turn, the managing director and the supervisors were not allowed to speak, nor were the workers, but they could also pass each other written notes. The chairman of each team was given, simultaneously, the identical task to achieve, thereby creating something of a race against the other team but also against the dreaded "watch."

I had used this exercise perhaps a hundred times before, in England, the United States, Australia, New Zealand, Italy, and elsewhere. Over a twenty-year period, no team had ever solved the problem within the time limit, and the purpose of the exercise was to create data (behavior) that could be debated afterward to examine why teams fail. The route cause of the failure is often because the chairman does not explain the task to his or her managing director but starts issuing instructions. The result is that he or she is the only one who knows what the company is trying to achieve; everyone else is clueless, so they start creating their own agendas or get frustrated.

With these groups described, I found myself with two teams, one of which had a black chairman and a black managing director. To my utter amazement, within ten minutes of the task being set, the black chairman put up her hand and announced that her team had solved the problem. I must admit that I thought it was a fluke. However, the next week I conducted the same exercise with two more groups of trainees and, to my delight, the same thing happened. One of the new groups also had a black chairman, but this time an

Asian managing director. Sure enough, this group also solved the problem within the time limit, proving to me, beyond all reasonable doubt, that these results were not flukes.

The lesson was not that black chairpersons are capable of solving problems better than white ones. The lesson came from what followed. In both cases, when the twelve trainees returned to the classroom for the debriefing I was able to tell them that they were the first people in history to solve the problem. I told them that they had succeeded where the English, the Americans, the Aussies, and so on, had failed. Broad beams of pride spread across their faces and, from that moment on, the confidence levels of all twelve trainees became so high that they sailed through the rest of the course in superb style and went back to their daily supervisory jobs with newfound confidence and success. Africans have often been told that they are the basket case of the world. If you tell people something often enough, they will begin to believe you. If you can create confidence in them to perform, they will continue to surprise you.

I know this because the same thing happened to me as a very young assistant manager. Through a slice of good luck, I was selected to participate in one of the first T groups to be held in Europe. T groups were also known as Sensitivity Training Groups. They work in the following way: A group of individuals, normally no more than ten, is brought together for a minimum five-day training session. This group of strangers gathers on the first day (or normally evening) with the trainer or trainers. The expectancy of the group is that the trainer will do what trainers normally do; that is, explain the goals and format of the upcoming training program. However, in this case, the trainer does nothing; she says nothing and she does nothing, leaving, of course, a horrible vacuum, which the assembled trainee group starts to fill with somewhat nervous behavior. The group, having been denuded of its expectant leadership (the trainer), starts to take on a life form of its own, which can be both fascinating and stressful. Natural leaders emerge, grow strong, and fail. Some manipulate, others sit on the sidelines, and so on. Eventually everyone finds a role, and a strong team with strong bonds emerges, not, I might say, without a good deal of drama along the way.

The group that I found myself in was both impressive and intimidating. I was only twenty-three years old; the next youngest participant was, perhaps, in his mid forties. The rest were either professors of psychology or captains of industry. I was a lowly assistant manager of a hotel. To say that I felt overwhelmed and nervous was an understatement. However, upon retiring to my room on the first night, I asked myself what I had to lose? After all, I considered, this situation must be equally strange to all of the other chaps, and, upon reflection, they had far more to lose than me. They were all important people; they wouldn't want to look foolish. I was unimportant. Why not just be myself and see what happened?

The result was astounding. As the week progressed, I learned that these captains of industry and boffins were also human beings, just like me. Stripped of their "office" and titles, denuded of their personal assistants, and tossed into this strange environment, they became ordinary human beings. They displayed their competitive or aggressive natures to each other and, in some cases, their compassion. None of them, however, had any reason to be competitive or aggressive to me, from whom they had nothing to fear. The strange result was that I was able to take the role of mediator, father confessor, peacemaker, and, in a round-about way, leader. As such, I gained their respect and, by the end of the week, they gained respect for each other. Eventually the group became a team and I had not been relegated to the bench; I was as important a member of the team as anyone else. I left the group with renewed confidence. I had proved to myself that I could swim with the sharks. It was a life-changing experience, and the confidence has never left me, just as I hope it never leaves my African trainees.

Tip 82: Lead by example.
Role modeling.

An interesting trend has been occurring over the past ten years in the London restaurant scene. The focus has shifted from good service to good cuisine. When I was a trainee in a restaurant, the restaurant manager, or maitre'd, was as important, if not more important, than the chef. Very often, restaurant clientele would not even know the name of the chef, even in the best establishments, but they almost certainly would know the name of the manager. Restaurants tended to be called by the name of the owner or restaurateur, who was normally the front-of-house man, not the man in the back. Harry of Harry's Bar was not the chef! As a result, the service in the best establishments was always impeccable. Plates were served from the right and cleared from the left, ladies were served before gentlemen, the sommelier did not reach over the table to pour the wine, place settings were always set out with military precision etc. Why? Because the maitre'd would insist. He would walk the room with beady eyes, making sure that nothing about the service would upset "his" guests. He would be personally immaculate, with shiny shoes and a crisp shirt and suit. He would be ingratiatingly polite to his guests. He was, of course, a role model to his employees. The quality of the food, however, did not always match up to its billing, and London was certainly not renowned as a gastronomic center.

Gradually there has been a shift. With the rise of the celebrity chef, with the importation of great Continental talent, and with the increasing interest in good food and wine among the public, the kitchen has become more important than the dining room. Chefs now own restaurants, and many restaurants are now named after chefs rather than after restaurateurs. The role model, therefore, in these restaurants is no longer the maitre'd, but the chef. The result, of course, is that the quality of food served in London's top restaurants now rivals anywhere in the world. The quality of service, alas, does not. Food is no longer served; it arrives pre-plated. Men are frequently served before women. Nobody cares if the knife is not lined up with the fork, and service staff is no longer deferential but often exceptionally casual and sloppy. Would I rather have it this way? I suppose. But would I prefer it if the food had improved and the service had not slipped? Of course I would.

What it demonstrates is the power of role modeling. You have probably heard the expression "Don't listen to what I say, listen to what I mean!" A similar expression could be "Don't do what I tell you to do, do what I do!" We are the product, to a large degree, of our environment, and those whom we respect, look up to, or report to make up a dominant part of that environment. It is irrefutable that the behavior of the parent affects the behavior of the child, and unless the child can consciously break the pattern of behavior that has been demonstrated, he will, in one way or another, make the same mistakes as the parent. The same is true for the boss. If the boss is lazy, or deskbound, or autocratic, there is the strong chance that the employee will engage in like behavior. A hotel manager who spends little or no time with his guests cannot expect his employees to bother with them either. Take an example I have used before. If you are in a staff meeting with your boss, which is interrupted by a secretary, who is fending off a guest, but the response from the manager is to tell the secretary that he cannot be disturbed because he is in a meeting, guess what? That is exactly what the average assistant manager will do, too. On the other hand, if, like George DeKornfeld, the manager, sometimes to the annoyance of the gathered meeting, is willing to interrupt the meeting to meet the guest, this is exactly the behavior that will flow through his organization. This makes it sound as if we are all programmed zombies, but the sad truth is, that largely we are. Although the reverse may not be true, that if our boss is behaving badly, we automatically follow his example. However, the easiest route to take is to do so, for by not following the example, we open ourselves up to potential conflict with the boss, and although eventually productive, this course can be painful and stressful. Most employees are not prepared to go through the pain.

As managers, therefore, we must understand that it is no good telling our employees to do one thing and then do differently ourselves. If we genuinely believe that the standards we have set, and are busy training people to achieve, are important, then we must demonstrate them. If you are doing your rounds and come across some litter on the pathway, the best thing you can do is to pick it up. Don't make a note of it and ask someone else to pick it up later. You will be amazed how many of your staff will do likewise, if that is the example you have set. This behavior comes back to being there, or management by walking about. If as the manager, you are hidden from view, closeted in your office, or always on holiday during the peak periods, you will not be around to demonstrate the desired behavior. You cannot be a positive role model unless you can be seen. You cannot expect others to work hard if you are lazy. A common mistake that some people make is to think that once they have reached the exalted position of boss, they can put their feet on the table. I have run across many examples of people who have worked their socks off to get to the position of manager only to relax. Being manager is the hardest job of all and requires the most work.

Tip 83: Beware of the barriers.
Never mind the guest!

The organizational structure of a hotel (and many other businesses) is set up to fail. The jobs in a hotel have, of necessity, been departmentalized. The different functions performed by the personnel in each department require different skills, different training, and, in many cases, different types of people. The result is that each department tends to fence itself off from the next and, instead of being cooperative, becomes combative. Sometimes this is due to the personalities in charge of each department, and sometimes it occurs because of the nature of the work. Whatever the cause, this departmentalization creates barriers to communication and efficiency, with the result that there are winners and losers among departments. Normally the real loser, in these circumstances, is the guest or client.

I first learnt this many years ago when I was a commis waiter in a very formal restaurant at Grosvenor House, in Park Lane, London. In those days, the restaurant had a strict hierarchy. The restaurant manager greeted and seated the guests, the station head waiter explained the menu and took the orders, the chef de rang prepared the table with the correct cutlery and assisted the station head waiter in serving the food, and the commis de rang (me!) ran to the kitchen with the order and generally fetched and carried.

The kitchen had a different hierarchy. During the service, the head chef stood on the cool side of the pass, directing the kitchen like the conductor of an orchestra. The sous chef, assisted him, but when needed, went to the stoves to finish something or to correct a mistake or to season a dish to perfection. The chefs de parties organized the cooking at each station (i.e., sauce, vegetables, pastry) and the commis chefs did the prep work, fetched, and carried.

The organization barrier was that as the most junior person from the restaurant, I found myself giving the most senior person in the kitchen, an "order." Sure enough, it was not a personal order. It was the order that my local boss had taken from the customer; it was what the customer wanted. Nevertheless, I was the messenger, and in the hurly-burly and pressure that happens at service time in a kitchen, I was the messenger who frequently was shot. I can remember, on one occasion, that the customers at one of my tables had preordered a soufflé for dessert. Knowing that a soufflé takes some time to cook and knowing that a soufflé is best served immediately after it leaves the oven, I took it upon myself, by observing the progress my customers were making with their main course, to go in to the kitchen and tell the chef de cuisine to "put on the soufflé." "I'll put the fucking soufflé on when I want" came back the immediate response, "not when some fucking whippersnapper tells me!" With that, I slunk back to the restaurant and watched with annoyance my diners sitting around wondering why it took so long to serve the dessert.

These barriers to success are not confined to the restaurant and the kitchen. They proliferate throughout the hotel structure and are exacerbated by the personalities involved. Just as in the previous example, a similar situation exists between the front desk and the housekeeping department. One of the most junior members of staff, the desk clerk, is also at the sharp end of the business, facing the customer. His job is to receive the guests and to make sure that they are allocated and able to check in to the rooms they have reserved. In all hotels, departing guests obviously make way for arriving guests, but between the departure and the arrival, someone has to clean and prepare the room. The person in charge of this activity is the executive housekeeper, who directs the chambermaids, who are also at the sharp end. More often than not, departing guests tend to do so later than convenient and arriving guests tend to be earlier, resulting in the not-unusual situation that some guests have to wait for their rooms to be ready. The person who handles them during this wait is the lowly desk clerk. The person who controls the order in which rooms are cleaned, checked, and returned to the front desk is the executive housekeeper. Executive housekeepers do not always do things in the order that front desk clerks ask them to. They sometimes do not want to hear that it is the guest asking; they think it is the desk clerk telling.

When people put on their "uniforms," they tend to behave in ways that they feel are appropriate with the status conferred on them, or earned by them, through their right to wear the uniform. Police officers tend to behave as we would expect them to when they are on duty. The police uniform entitles the officer to behave with authority and the officer on duty is entitled to be treated with respect. When the officer is at home, he cannot expect to behave with the same authority and, if he does, he will probably not get much respect. People with titles tend to act out the expected role that the title confers on them. Chefs act like prima donnas, housekeepers act like headmistresses, and so on. Instead of acting reasonably in their dealings with other staff members wherever they sit on the hierarchy, in the interests of satisfying the needs of the guest, they tend to act in a manner that protects their turf and the importance of their position. What a manager needs to do is to break down these barriers to efficiency, and one way to do this is through behavioral and organizational development training.

Tip 84: Change behavior and behavior will change.
Team building.

For a number of years in the late 1990s and early 2000s, Chelsea Football Club had some very talented players but never won the English Premier League championship. They consistently came in second or third or fourth but somehow, when the chips were down, they always disappointed. In the 2004–05 season, there was a management change and, in some fashion or other, the new manager Jose Mourinho, transformed the club from a collection of great players into a great team. I recently went to Stamford Bridge, their stadium, on a couple of occasions to watch them play. On one occasion, I sat in the second row, which at this stadium is very close to the action. I could not have been more impressed with what I saw; the players were giving their all, but they were giving it in support of each other. There was not one lazy or selfish player on the field. They ran and ran to cover for each other. They won both matches and, at the time of writing, are eleven points clear of any other team at the top to the league. Interestingly, looking at another league statistic, that of leading goal scorers, there is not one Chelsea player in the top six. Why? Because not one of the superstars is hogging the limelight; they have been sharing the goal-scoring opportunities; they have been playing as a team.

Possibly, Jose Mourinho would make a good hotel manager, because one of management's tasks is to get the superstars (departmental heads) to work as a team in order to win the match (make a profit by satisfying the guest). In this regard, I am able to relate two instances of how this has been achieved. The first was many years ago at the Carlton Tower Hotel in London. Following my experiences, as described earlier, on the T group, I decided to learn the skill (or art) of becoming a T group trainer. This training equipped me to handle groups of people, at all levels, in training sessions designed to get them to understand how they could help each other and learn from each other as human beings, rather than as "uniformed" operatives. The Carlton Tower was emerging from a period when the general manager, Antoine Dirsztay, had operated as if he were in charge of the Gestapo. Dirsztay managed by threats and fear, by divide and rule. As a result, the department heads were more intent on transferring blame when things went adrift and protecting their backsides than solving problems.

Antoine Dirsztay had, unfortunately for him, dropped dead on the tennis court, and was replaced by a kinder, gentler regime. Some of the old interdepartmental scars remained, and as personnel executive for the organization at the time, I suggested to the company that they allow me to run a series of mini T groups for all supervisory and management staff at the hotel, which numbered about seventy people. These included senior management, departmental heads, down to any supervisor who had anyone reporting to them.

The program I designed, with the help of my colleagues in Boston, was six days long. I divided the seventy people into groups of ten, selecting each group, not by department, but by taking a diagonal slice across the organization chart, thereby ensuring that at each training session there were people from a cross section of the hotel departments. A typical grouping would have been, say, the assistant manager F&B, the executive housekeeper, the shift leader from the front desk, the person in charge of night cleaning, the chief electrician, and so on. I decided to conduct the training sessions away from the hotel and rented a small ramshackle country hotel with exactly the right number of bedrooms to accommodate my groups. I scheduled the seven training sessions to run, more or less, back to back. The groups were asked to focus on the problems that they ran into in trying to perform their duties at work, to examine the reasons for these problems, and to come up with solutions. Many of the problems related to easily resolved issues, such as lack of operating equipment and the like, but most came down to an appalling lack of cooperation between the departments and a lack of understanding of the challenges and difficulties facing each department. At first, of course, the junior supervisors were somewhat inhibited by the senior ones, but slowly, just as had happened to me in my original T group, the participants became human beings, not supervisors. The seniors began to see that the juniors had something to teach them, and the juniors began to understand how the scars of life had affected the seniors. Finally, everybody agreed that if they could work in harmony, and with mutual respect, the winners would ultimately be the hotel guests.

Week by week my training groups returned to the Carlton Tower, breathing goodwill to each other. Initially, those who had yet to attend the "training" were highly skeptical and scathing. Gradually, as the number of supervisors who had attended the sessions outweighed those who had not, the atmosphere back at the hotel changed dramatically, until the final trainees returned to the warm welcome of all of those who had preceded them. If ever a program produced behavioral change, this was it. The efficiency of the hotel improved beyond recognition, occupancy figures and profits rose and staff turnover declined to almost zero.

Behavior change programs are worthwhile only if the change is for the better and is permanent. If you manage to get someone to change a negative behavior into a positive one, it has to be something they have decided they want to do, and something they receive positive reinforcement for once they have changed. The more someone practices a new and better behavior, the more it becomes his or her normal behavior and, if it is applauded by colleagues and reaps positive results, the person will be even happier about it. I recently ran across a participant from those days, now retired, who told me that the Carlton Tower was the happiest place he had ever worked.

Another route to building successful teams is to involve employees, at all levels, in setting the goals for the business. Every business should have core values, an understanding of what things are important to the business, and what makes it special. A set of core values is not something that you inject into staff or instruct them to carry out. These values need to be things that the supervisors and staff understand and want to achieve or abide by. One way to arrive at this happy state of affairs is to let the staff build the core values with you. This exercise can be done in much quicker fashion than a behavioral change program. It is really team building through a buy-in, that is a buy-in to the basic values of the business. To achieve this, it is necessary to bring together as many management and supervisors as you can for two days without negatively affecting the business. Through a program of explaining the process to participating in the subject matter, you will be able to reach a consensus on what can make your business special. You will need to give everybody air time in a disciplined fashion, and then, work steadily through the ideas to achieve agreement. Having done so, you can challenge all participants to pledge to you what they will do in the future to make sure that the company runs in accordance with the agreed values.

Tip 85: Manage from the bottom up.
Trusting your workers.

A big mistake that managers make is to assume that their employees are dummies and, as a result, need to be spoon-fed. Once employees are confident in their environment and their ability to do the job (i.e., after proper induction and job content training), they are ready to contribute to the success of the job in their own special and individual ways. Many of your employees are in the front end of the business, dealing with your customers or directly servicing those who are. Once you are satisfied that the basic technical standards you have set are being followed, you should leave room for innovation. You will be surprised how innovative employees can be.

We have all experienced the member of staff who is carrying out the company instructions by rote. "Have a good day!" or "The One and Only Royal Mirage, may I help you?" It doesn't sound sincere. When your people are dealing with your customers, let them be themselves, provided they are in accord with the core values. It is no good giving staff with a laundry list of catch phrases that they must recite for every guest contact interaction. It will seem phony. Instead, challenge your staff to come up with their own list for pleasing their guests. What is important is that your staff *wants* to please their customers, not that they have to.

When you observe or hear about outstanding examples of your employees' efforts to go beyond the call of duty to satisfy guests, reward them by thanking them and sharing their special ideas with others, so these ideas will spread through the organization by osmosis, not as a command to be resented.

Tip 86: Ban blame.
Empower your staff.

Recognize that your frontline staff in particular represent your company; in most cases, they are the only representatives that your customers will meet. If they have been properly trained and are properly managed, they will not deliberately go out of their way to upset your guests; the chances are it will be the reverse. But things will go wrong and guests' problems will need to be sorted out. Or, customers' questions or demands will have to be met. The double baggers in your organization, in most instances, will, if allowed, be capable of solving the problems or effecting "recovery" on the spot. Instant and rapid solutions to guest problems are exactly what your customers are seeking. "Would you mind taking a seat while I contact the manager?" or "The manager is in a meeting now, but I will ask him to deal with the matter later" are not what a guest wants to hear. So why not empower your frontline staff to make decisions, which could include such things as offering not to charge for unsatisfactory service or extending a checkout time? You can set limits, of course, but 90 percent of the problems will fall away within very reasonable limits.

When all of your employees have the same passion as you, provided they have been properly trained, the risks of anyone making the sort of recovery decision that will break the bank are minimal. A good manager will encourage his staff to make decisions. Nothing stops him later reviewing the decisions and counseling the staff member on the quality of that decision. This, however, does not mean that a manager is free to reprimand or blame the staff member after the event. If you have created a culture in which your employees are empowered to make decisions, then you will also have to accept that they will, from time to time, make the wrong ones, just as you do. If they run the risk of being blamed for incompetence or stupidity when they screw up, they will never make a decision, on the company's behalf, again. A company operating under a culture of blame will be dysfunctional; smooth operations will clog up, and the natural barriers within the organization will become walls with barbed wire on top. Ideas will remain just ideas and will never bubble up into meaningful contributions to the service and the bottom line. Fertilize your employees so that they grow; don't keep them in the dark so that they wither away.

10

Controlling the Assets

Tip 87: *Count on your controller.*
The importance of proper bookkeeping.

Now that you have built and opened your hotel, and trained, motivated, and empowered your staff, you had better figure out how to hang on to the loot. There are three ways to keep control of your assets: through paper and data, through people, and through seeing for yourself what is going on. Your assets include fixed assets, cash, stocks, and your human resources. In this chapter, I discuss the control of these assets, other than people. But, as always, to do so effectively, you will find yourself relying on people.

The backbone of fiscal control is management information, and the foundation of this is proper bookkeeping. Without proper bookkeeping, you have no chance at all of controlling or managing your business. Unless you have a proper record of every single transaction that takes place in your business, you may never know what exactly is going on, and you will be wide open to waste and, even worse, robbery.

The oddly named profit and loss statement should be a summary of every revenue that you have recorded over a specific period and every expenditure. Since the idea of being in business is to make a profit, if you subtract the expenditures from the revenues, you hope there will be a profit and not a loss. (You won't stay in business long if you continually make a loss, so I cannot understand why we don't call this set of accounts by the rather more optimistic title of profit statement.) The balance sheet, which is normally produced along with the P&L statement, is not a trading statement, but one that reflects the current value of your businesses' assets and its short and long-term liabilities.

In order for the P&L statement to be meaningful, it must be accurate and produced in sufficient detail for you, the manager, to be able to understand what parts of the business are performing well and which, if any, are not. To some degree, specifically as it reflects upon the business's tax liability, there are rules and regulations about how you must account. The purpose of producing a P&L statement is not, however, primarily to satisfy tax man, but to provide management with data. You are, therefore, free to record your revenue and expenditures in as much or as little detail as you like, but it is wise to do so in a consistent manner that allows you to make meaningful comparisons with past performance and like businesses. Fortunately, over the years, the global hotel and catering industry has developed a standardized format for accounts, known as the Uniform System. This system prescribes to which line account every type of revenue should be posted, as well as every type of expenditure. For example, toilet rolls are expendable items and should be charged to the rooms division under the category of "guest supplies," unless, of course, a smart bookkeeper can demonstrate that they were all used in the restaurant toilets, in which case there would be a case for charging them as "restaurant supplies." To allocate expenditure, a system of recording the "life" of every item must be introduced, from the day it is ordered, through delivery, storage, transfer to an operational department, and consumption. By definition, this means a lot of paper or electronic records, and a lot of careful allocation and posting. This task must be performed with great diligence. If it is not, the management accounts will be meaningless and you will lose control of your business.

A hotel manager, therefore, relies heavily on the effectiveness of his controller or accountant, who must be capable of installing the detailed systems that are required to achieve proper accountability and making sure that they are always followed. To be effective, the controller must be separated from the hustle of dealing with the guests, except insofar as making sure that guest bills are properly presented and that guests actually pay promptly what they owe. As previously mentioned, the position of controller is so important that in many hotel organizational structures, especially years ago, it ranked as equal to that of the hotel manager. Being separated from the sharp end of the business means that, once again, there is potential for an interdepartmental barrier, with the possibility that service will suffer. For example, if the accountant insists that the chef cannot remove goods from the storeroom without a written requisition, and this requisition causes a delay in a guest receiving, say, some Beluga caviar, a row could ensue between the headwaiter, the chef, and the accountant, and, ultimately, the guest, who since she is ordering caviar, is probably an important one. It is, therefore, the duty of the accountant to set up the systems to have the minimum negative impact on the guests, and to make sure that she explains to everyone how they can best avoid such impact, by proper planning and organization. Life, unfortunately, does not always work this way.

Bookkeepers sometimes need to stand firm. They are the guardians of your assets. It is not normally too difficult for the rest of your employees to understand why the bookkeepers must insist on fiscal controls. After all, each employee will be able to understand why he or she would not want other people dipping into personal bank accounts without prior authority. Sometimes, however, bookkeepers are unnecessarily intransigent, and this is when a spot of team training is required. It is no good trying to speed along on the passion train if someone has their hands permanently on the break.

Bookkeepers and accountants can also be dishonest, which is like having to deal with dishonest police officers. To ensure against this, conduct regular audits carried out by specialists outside accounting firms. These audits will not only provide you with a useful scorecard, evaluating the effectiveness of your controls, but will also help keep your bookkeeper honest. In my career, I have run across three accountants who were robbing the business. In each case, they managed to do so for a long time before they tripped up. On reflection, they all had a common trait. They worked so impressively hard that they hardly ever took a day off or a vacation. At the time, I put it down to double bagging, but I was wrong; they didn't want anyone else to get a good look at the books.

Tip 88: Keep the banks at bay.
The importance of liquidity.

I recently read a newspaper report about a well-known British television newscaster who was being sued by a credit card company for a $45,000 debt. The poor woman, it turned out, was not so poor. She owned two or three apartments in London, as well as her home, but the rents were going to meet the mortgages and she had no cash. She had plenty of equity in the homes but couldn't sell them easily due to the rental agreements. It seemed highly likely that she had, in fact, overleveraged her position. Obviously, the newspaper did not go into the intricate details of her financial affairs, but it did bring home to me the point that cash is king. You can have all of the illiquid assets in the world, but if you don't have any cash and your credit has run out, you won't be able to pay the bus fare or the grocery bill.

When property and real estate prices are rising, there is a great temptation to borrow heavily against your assets. After all, anyone can see that if you borrow 100 percent of the purchase price to buy a house that doubles in value over time, then you will have a massive return for no investment at all, save for the interest you will need to pay on the loan, that is, of course, if you have any cash to so do. There is also a great temptation for hoteliers to over-leverage their businesses for the same reason. This is terrific while the hotel is going well, with strong occupancies and high rates, but is very dangerous if the business cannot throw off enough cash. Remember, the hotel business tends to be cyclical. In any one location or region, people tend to invest in hotels when there is a shortage of rooms. Often different developers recognize the shortage at the same time, with the result that several new products are brought to the market simultaneously. This positively affects the supply of hotel rooms, but negatively affects occupancies and rates because suddenly, oversupply of the product turns a sellers' market into a buyers' market. If you are unlucky enough to have borrowed heavily against the value of your property while you had plenty of cash flow to meet the repayments, but are now faced with a downturn in business of such magnitude that you can no longer finance the loan, the result will be, that the bank will now own your hotel. Eventually the cycle may change as demand continues to grow, but this advantage will now accrue to the bank. As a rule of thumb, never borrow more than 50 percent of the value of your hotel. This might seem cautious, but at least it will still be your hotel.

Another important aspect to maintaining good cash flow is to make sure that you collect the money you are owed. In theory, a hotel is paid in cash for services rendered and credit should be limited to guaranteed arrangements with credit card companies. In practice, this can be different, particularly in connection with travel trade accounts and, in some cases, banqueting or corporate clients. Wholesale travel companies collect the money from their clients (your guests) well in advance of their travel dates. Most hotel companies allow the wholesale travel companies thirty days to pay. This means, of course, that the travel company has someone else's money, both your guests' and yours, for two months, and in some cases, they make more money through bank interest than from reservation commissions. This is acceptable to most hotels because the volume of business supplied by the wholesalers makes it all worthwhile, unless, of course, they go broke, before you get your hands on the money. It is, therefore, of vital importance that you frequently review the state of your debtors and, should any account go past thirty days' due, no matter how good a client he or she may have been in the past, you must pursue payment aggressively. Your biggest weapon, of course, if this is a regular client, is to refuse entry to the next scheduled arrival, on the basis that you will not add to their debt burden.

Take care also, that the invoices you present to your debtors are accurate and faultless. We all know the trick of holding up payment because the actual invoice is slightly incorrect, with the wrong date, or wrong room number, or even a misspelled name!

Tip 89: Get what you pay for.
Prudent purchasing.

Purchasing is a big subject that demands, like many other subjects in this book, more comment and consideration than can reasonably be given in a *Hundred Tips for Hoteliers*. What can be stated, however, is that approximately 30 percent of your revenues will be expended regularly on buying goods for eventual resale, without even considering the purchasing of equipment that is not for resale. Paying 10 percent too much, for whatever reason, on daily purchases, could reduce your bottom line profit by 3 percent. In plain words, if your revenues in a hundred-room, four-star hotel are, say, $10 million per annum, you could be losing $300,000 through faulty purchasing, or stated differently, someone in your organization might be pocketing $300,000. It is, therefore, important for your organization to narrow the field of opportunity for dishonest purchasing as much as possible.

One way is to channel all purchasing through one trusted and reliable purchasing officer, with sufficient checks and balances to keep him honest. If you allow the chef and the housekeeper to do their own departmental purchasing instead, you will open the door for all sorts of temptation, which could result in not only losing money but ultimately suffering from poor-quality goods and delivery. Also, chefs should concentrate on what they have been trained to do; negotiation is probably not one of those things. Understanding quality is, without doubt, part of a chef's remit, but this can be achieved through his right to specify what he needs and to refuse to accept anything less. He does not have to place the actual order.

Not all poor purchasing comes about as the result of a supplier rewarding the purchaser; some is due to procedural inefficiency, and here, the hotel manager can keep her eyes and ears open to prevent it as she manages by walking around. It does no harm for a manager, from time to time, to stop at the delivery dock and personally check a specific delivery to see that it is of the quality specified and in the right quantity. Short delivery is one of the easiest ways to be robbed. A supplier soon gets to know which hotels check what is received and which receiving clerks are honest. Often tricks are played with part delivery techniques, which confuse the paperwork. It is up to your staff to keep the supplier honest; it is up to you to make sure that your staff realizes that you are watching. You must ensure that you get what you pay for.

Tip 90: Stop the chicken run.
Keep stocks low.

You must also make sure that your purchaser is receiving competitive bids and, from time to time, it is worthwhile listening to the gripes of a losing bidder, although he may be a sore loser. Do not be tempted to buy too much. Make sure your purchaser keeps the storerooms as empty as possible. Stocks tie up your cash and earn no interest. When a supplier tries to interest you in taking a truckload of prawns because they are half price, take care. Prawns in your deep freeze will not earn you any money and will be difficult to control. As you walk about your hotel, it will be very easy for you to figure out if someone has stolen a chicken, if there are only two chickens in the freezer. If there are a hundred chickens there, you will never know if one has gone walkabout.

When I worked as a commis waiter in the 1960s, some of my colleagues were always anxious to take the cheese trolley back to the fridges at the close of service. Running along the wall outside and above the fridge doors were some large service pipes. The commis depositing the cheese would, as a matter of course, steal a chicken and lob it above the pipes outside the fridge door when no one was looking. Having returned to his cleanup duties in the restaurant, he would wait for the senior waiters to leave before sauntering, homeward bound, through the kitchen. As he passed the fridge door, a deft little jump was enough for him to snatch the chicken and shove it under his jacket. I guarantee that the chef never knew he'd lost a chicken.

And while thinking about storerooms, it is not a bad idea, no matter how inconvenient it may be, to change the locks frequently. For people who are determined to steal from you, it will not take them long to acquire a key. If they keep finding they have the wrong key, it could become a little frustrating.

Unfortunately for hoteliers, almost everything they are likely to keep in or out of the storerooms is likely to be useful at home for most of their employees. Food and beverage to tableware and linen all make attractive targets for disgruntled or nefarious staff. Obviously, most of your employees will not fall into this category, but there will, alas, be a few who will qualify, and you must make it as difficult as possible for them. First, you need to know if you are being robbed. If the robbery is one "drip" at a time, like the nightly chicken, you may never be alerted to the problem, but at least it will be a small one. One way that you can find out about leakage is to take stock frequently and randomly. If the consumption does not make sense in conjunction with your sales or reasonable usage estimates, or experience, you will need to investigate.

A few years ago, the manager of Le Galawa Beach Hotel in the Comores told me that he had been invited to the Grand Mariage ceremony of one of his employee's daughters. A Grand Mariage in the Comores is, as its name implies, a grand occasion for which proud parents will use up their life savings. This ceremony and reception took place in a rural village where the employee lived. To the manager's amazement he found the outdoor dinner table, which was set for close to sixty people, was completely equipped with the hotel's flatware, hollowware, and linen. When he expressed surprise to his host, he told him that he had every right to use it, because he had bought it all in the local market. One can only assume that the manager's stocktaking or security was not very effective.

Tip 91: Look after the paper clips.
Avoid waste.

The chair of Bear Stearns in New York wrote a bestseller called *Memos from the Chairman*. One chapter was titled, "Look after the paper clips and the profits will look after themselves." In his business, paper clips, as well as paper itself, are important. Nobody believed, however, that saving paper clips and paper would have a huge impact on the bottom line at Bear; what would make a difference was the spirit of waste avoidance, which, if built into the culture of Bear, could go a long way to contributing to bigger profits.

Waste avoidance is even more relevant to a hotel because there are so many ways that waste can occur and, thus, be prevented. The most important factor here is to make sure that your staff focuses on this, just as Abe tried to do at Bear. Each individual instance of waste or breakage may seem insignificant to a member of staff but it is easy to demonstrate just how quickly all of the waste items add up. As a manager, once again, you need to be a role model in this regard; by being there, you will have plenty of opportunity to demonstrate your interest in this subject. As you go on your rounds, from time to time, ask for the garbage at the back door to be tipped out and sorted through. You will be amazed what you will find. As you walk on the floors, look at what is left on the room service trays. It is always very informative to see what a guest could not consume and to wonder why. For example, look at the size of the milk jug on a tray for one person's coffee or tea. Chances are you will find the same size jug being used as if for two or more persons, with the result that half of the milk is being wasted. Ditto for sugar and butter and all of the other little extras that go on to a tray.

Look in the maids' cupboards or in the drawers in the offices. If they are not neat, clean, and tidy, you know that they are signals for waste. Check the phone bills and relate them to actual phone sets. Investigate the actual numbers called from each phone; it will be very revealing. If you see recurring numbers, dial them; you will probably find yourself talking to a stockbroker, bookie, or somebody's girlfriend. Get one of your computer people to check the number of hits from the myriad of computers that you are bound to have in the business, and you will probably find that the most hits are connected to sport or porn. It is interesting that some managers feel that they are infringing their employees' rights by checking up on these things, because the employees are not actually stealing anything. In my view, they are stealing; you are paying them and they are stealing your time.

The important thing about the manager's noting all of these little items of waste while on his rounds is for him to stop bad practices before they take root. It may be possible to identify waste from an analysis of expenditures versus budget in the monthly profit statement, but this is *after* the event. Seeing waste firsthand gives you the chance to stop it way before the monthly accounts appear on your desk.

Tip 92: Zero in on your budget.
Budgeting as a management tool

The best control tool you can ever have will be through your budget, provided the budget has been produced with the proper care, thought, and focus. It is not uncommon for most hotel managers, with a higher authority to report to, to pad their budgets to give themselves room for error. If you are asking a manager to produce a budget for you to review, you will need to flush out where the padding is in order to get a true reading of the state and potential of the business.

The proper way to compile a budget is line by line and take each line back to zero. The lazy and inefficient way to prepare a budget is to take last year's figures and add an inflation factor. All that you are doing is to entomb and accept last year's inefficiencies.

By going back to zero, you ignore what has gone before and work out from scratch what revenues and expenditures really ought to be. Take our old friend, "rooms' guest supplies." To build up this line in the budget, you will need to examine every item that goes into this category. For the sake of this example, let us assume that there is only one item (there are, of course, many more): soap. You will now need to understand the standard to which you are operating the hotel in regard to soap. If, for instance, your policy is to provide a fresh wrapped soap brick every day to rooms that are already occupied, rather than leave the guest with the soap he has already partially used, then you will have to examine the size and cost of each bar of soap and, having decided that you are willing to continue with these items, multiply them by the number of guest nights you are anticipating in this budget. Having worked out what the cost of soap ought to be, you will probably get a shock when you compare this figure with what was actually spent the year before. This will almost certainly lead you, as part of the budget exercise, to examine such things as how the soap is bought, stored, issued, and controlled. If you do this thoroughly, the very task of trying to prepare a budget will already be leading you to better control practices.

When preparing a budget you will need to involve the relevant team players responsible for its achievement. You can do this on a department-by-department basis so that the whole supervisory structure is not tied up in one long meeting. You will find this process quite enlightening and will learn much about each individual's grasp on his or her job. Don't believe everything you are told, and don't expect everyone to have the answers to your questions at their fingertips; that would not be fair. Preparing a back to zero budget can be interesting for all parties concerned.

For example, assume that you have four restaurants in a hotel and that the hotel manager reports to you. You could start by asking the manager or the food and beverage manager how much is charged for coffee in each venue. They will probably give different answers. Even if they don't, you should ask someone for a menu/price list from each outlet. You will probably discover that there are at least four different prices being charged for coffee (maybe with good reason), that they are all different from the ones stated by management, and that they haven't been adjusted for two years. Right there, the budget process will have given you an opportunity to increase profits, albeit in a tiny way. However, the study of the menus and the comparisons with each other might throw up a whole host of other pricing opportunities that have escaped the attention of management in the hustle of everyday service. They might also demonstrate that, in some instances, the price is too high and, hence, the sales are too low.

Use the budget process to focus on every category of revenue and expenditure with fresh eyes. In most hotels, it is a job that will take at least a couple of days. If it is not possible, due to time constraints, to examine every line, don't take the route of skipping through all of them superficially. Choose a limited number and examine them in detail; at least this will set a tone for the people involved and create a mindset of always challenging the facts as they appear.

The biggest single expense that you are likely to have is payroll, and it is certainly worth taking extra time to examine in detail the number of staff and their remuneration, and all of the perquisites that will have crept in over the years. Perks, which are often handed out on a once-off basis, have a habit of becoming a permanent and expected feature, or a "right." Whether it is free parking or staff taking three meals per day when they are only entitled to two, or food deliveries to the manager's house, existing practices must be uncovered and approved, or discontinued. The number of employees must also be scrutinized. Payrolls have a habit of creeping up not down. Jobs, which are sometimes no longer necessary, have a habit of remaining. Some jobs could be combined without any undue strain on the organization. This is not just a desk review. Walk around, ask questions, and examine the job on-the-job. I will be surprised if you are not surprised.

If you are confident that you have created a thorough budget, it will, going forward, be a firm foundation on which to manage. If the revenues and expenses begin to flow through the business in line with this budget, you can be confident that the business is under control. If, however, certain actual results are at variance with the budget, you can also be sure that something has changed or gone wrong (or right) and needs investigating. The problems will leap off the page. You will know exactly where to focus your energies and where, if necessary, to instigate corrective action.

The best budget in the world, however, will be completely redundant if you don't have any data for comparison. In other words, the bookkeeping must be supplying you with information concerning actual revenue and expenses as promptly as possible. Don't wait for final or audited figures. Set up a system of "flash" reports to indicate where there may be potential problems that you will recognize as variances from your sound budget. The sooner you can get information, the sooner you can act on it.

Tip 93: Don't let them know when you're coming.
Maintain an element of surprise.

Many robberies take place after the burglar has "cased the joint." Burglary is not usually a spur-of-the-moment activity. It is planned. The targeted premises are kept under surveillance for some time, so the burglars can decide just when and how to carry out their work with the least possible risk. They are helped by the fact that most people tend to operate with a strong element of routine.

It is not a good idea, from the aspect of control, for a hotel manager to operate in a completely routine fashion. I am not suggesting you leap about interfering with and unsettling your staff, but don't restrict yourself to scheduled visits. Your personal relationship with your subordinates should be such that they view any visit as a positive and helpful event, not a threatening one. Nevertheless, unscheduled questions, phone calls, or visits tend to keep people sharp. It is, to some extent, human nature to relax a little when the boss has gone home. From an early age, we learned, "When the cat's away, the mice will play."

If your premises include, say, a nightclub or disco that has a cover charge, it would do no harm to pay the odd unannounced visit and count the number of people you see. You may be surprised to see how many covers were paid when you read your revenue report the next day.

11

Only Seven Tips to Go

My last few tips are more general in nature; they represent some of the more important lessons I have learned from forty-six years in the business. Some of them I learned the hard way. In many cases, I have been guilty of not following my own advice, to the cost of my own family. Nevertheless, they are lessons to be learned; maybe you will heed them better than I have.

Tip 94: Keep your feet on the ground.
Don't become the guest.

Hotel managers are rarely born with silver spoons in their mouths. They are more likely to have come from humble or middle-class backgrounds. In fact, the choice of hotel management as a career, was, and still is, to an extent, rather looked down upon by many educators and parents. It is regarded, in some countries, as a rather servile occupation, whereas, in others, it is seen as an option of last resort. You know the sort of thing, "Well, James is not much good at math or science or computing, so the best thing he can do is go into something less demanding, like hotel management." Yeah, right!

A mistake, which hotel managers often make, maybe as a result of their backgrounds, is to acquire a taste for what their customers like, and, indeed, to start satisfying that taste. Don't be fooled by the bright lights of the business. They are there to dazzle your customers, not to frazzle your mind. It is, of course, as we've discussed, important to socialize with your clients; it is not necessary to take on their habits. Remember, as part of your job, you are helping your customers enjoy their playtime. Remember, also, that they have probably earned the right to have a playtime, by working elsewhere, possibly very hard. If your guests are having a good time in your establishment, they are doing it on their vacation or time off. You must not, by joining in with them, fall into the trap of being on permanent vacation yourself. If you were the manager of a widget factory, it would be hard for you to have a lot of fun with widgets. Because the tools of your trade include food, booze, and beds, don't be tempted to mix your work with your pleasure. If you are inclined to "mess," don't do it on your own doorstep, just because all of the facilities and opportunities are readily available. Remember, you are the role model.

You are probably in a position of getting favors from guests or travel partners. But, keep in mind, there is no such thing as a free lunch. Someone will always expect something in return. This is particularly true if you are involved with sales or marketing, where you will be tempted to accept "freebies," often involving personal travel opportunities. Once you have accepted, you are hooked. One day the favor will be called in and you will probably be asked to respond with free rooms. They are, most likely, not yours to give away!

And beware of Greeks bearing gifts. During your career, you may find that you are tempted to accept a little "help" from someone when you are in a position to sign a deal or offer a contract. Apart from being unethical and immoral, this is the slippery road to disaster. Don't be naïve; we all have to face the fact that corruption exists. Corruption is, however, the biggest enemy of efficiency. Corruption is also a cell from which you cannot escape.

Tip 95: Stick to straight shooting.
Treat people as you want to be treated.

One day, shortly after Nelson Mandela's release from prison, we were honored to have him come to our house for dinner. He arrived with a driver and a security guard. As soon as we had exchanged greetings and invited him into the lounge, he very politely asked if it would be possible to feed his small entourage.

"Of course," I responded, "I will make sure that they get something."

"It will be the same as we are having?" he asked, not so much as a request but more as an instruction.

Despite the fact that this seriously mucked up our planned portions, I was impressed that this wonderful man's first priority was the well-being of his employees.

President Mandela was right. People want to be, and should be, treated fairly. They also want to be treated honestly. Employees do not mind hearing the truth, even if the truth is unpleasant or difficult. We all possess this sixth sense to feel when people are not being straight with us. It is stupid to lie to people. If this becomes a pattern of your behavior, people will not ever believe what you say, and you will never keep track of what you have said and will sooner or later get caught. Employees do not respect bosses who are not straight with them; employees do not work hard for those that they cannot respect.

Being honest with people can be particularly difficult if they are honestly doing their level best to perform but are failing. You must, in these circumstances, try to understand their problems and try to help them. But sometimes people are just not cut out to do what is expected of them in a particular job. It is not in the interests of these people to brush this under the carpet. It is far fairer to confront it even if it means the person loses his job. I have quite often, unfortunately, been in the position of having to let people go because they were failing. It is not as hard as it seems, because most people who are failing know that they are, and when you relieve them of the burden of trying, it is like lifting a heavy weight from their backs. I am still good friends with several people that I have fired. Looking back on the experience, they were grateful; they all went on to other things at which they were better and happier.

Avoid making promises to employees that you cannot honor. There is often a temptation to tell a subordinate that there is a better job for him around the corner, if he will just keep going in the difficult (and important to you) job that he is doing. It will not take long for the employee to realize that you are just stringing him along for your own benefit. You have a far better chance of keeping him where you want him if you tell him that he is doing an important job for you where he is, and you have no realistic hope of moving him now. At least he knows where he stands, and that is what people need to know. Once you have made a promise that you cannot keep, you will break the bond of trust between yourself and your employee. This bond will not be easily mended.

Avoid being neutral. If you are required to make a decision by an employee, then make one. Even if it turns out to be the wrong one, your employee will respect the fact that you offered strong direction. Everyone makes mistakes, including the boss, and everyone understands that. But when you make a mistake, stand up and be counted; take the rap. If you are the team leader and you lose the match, don't blame the team. Do not pass the blame onto your employees or colleagues. If you do, you will not have many of them for long. Remember the old maxim, "You meet the same people on the way up as you do on the way down." Never was a saying so pregnant with meaning, and it comes home to you when you retire. Much of life is about power. When you are a managing director, or manager, or supervisor, you have power over others. Remember that one day, when through age or ill health or poor performance, you will lose that power, and it will pass to others, possibly to people who used to work for you. A friend who retired about a year ago told me how strange it felt that the phone never rang any more. One wonders how he treated his colleagues and staff—or maybe they were just too busy concentrating on their newfound power.

Your best bet as a manager is to build a strong team around you. Do not be fearful of people who are after your job. Celebrate the fact. If you surround yourself with people who are so weak that they could never take your job, you probably won't keep it very long anyway. Get and keep the strongest people you can around you. One of them will inevitably get your job, but he might still be working for you, and, when you eventually retire at the top of the tree, he might still invite you for dinner.

Tip 96: Stand up to bullies.
The guest is not always right.

You will encounter a lot of bullies along the way; people who won't stop until they get what they want, no matter whom they trample. These people think they are always right and have a complete disregard for others. Greedy people. Selfish people. Someone must stand up to them. If you are unlucky enough to come across one in your organization, that someone must be you. Bullies can be stopped; they just need to come across someone who says no.

Don't think that all bullies are bosses. Sometimes they are your customers and they are bullying your staff. The customer is not always right, especially if he is a bully. One incident sticks in my mind. Many years ago, shortly after we had opened the Beacon Island Hotel, which had been a difficult experience for the manager, I was attending his New Year's Eve gala dinner. The Beacon Island Hotel was one of the first in the world with an atrium lobby. On this occasion, because of strong demand, the manager was using the lobby as an extra restaurant, which naturally placed a huge strain on the staff who had many more customers to cope with than normal. As the clock approached midnight, the staff and the manager were visibly exhausted. At this point, I spotted an irate guest gesticulating angrily toward the manager who appeared to be wilting under the attack. I went across to see what had happened. Apparently, a couple of youngsters, who should have been tucked up in bed, had mischievously tossed some pieces of soil from a planter in one of the upper corridor/balconies, into the lobby. These had unfortunately landed in the guest's champagne. The manager had apologized, offered replacement champagne, and by the time I reached the table, was almost groveling. The guest became increasingly abusive, not only to the consternation of the other diners but also to the fatigued staff in the area. It seemed to me that the manager had done all that he could under the circumstances, and after all, it was not exactly his fault. But the guest was a bully.

I intervened and was told, in no uncertain terms, by the guest that he would rather stay in a two-star motel than this, so-called five-star Beacon Island. "That's fine," I responded, quite calmly. "Then you shall have your way. I happen to know that they still have some rooms available at the Formosa Inn (a dump of a motel about two miles away). I shall arrange to have your belongings packed and will happily provide transport for you and your family there, right now." And I did. With the help of a couple of hovering security guards, I insisted that he leave. I saw the spirits of the hard-pressed manager and staff rise. At about noon the next day, I had a phone call from the Formosa Inn. The man didn't like the Formosa Inn. He was sorry for his rudeness and wondered if he could come back. "Of course," I responded with concealed triumph.

Tip 97: Don't go stale.
Shake it up, baby.

No matter how varied your life will be as a hotel executive, there is the risk that you will go stale. After all, walking your property day after day can become "just more of the same thing." I remember, a few years ago, leaning on a railing at the almost finished Sugar Beach Hotel in Mauritius, thinking, "not another hotel opening!" and deciding that it would be my last. It wasn't to be, but at the time, I realized that I had become stale. Opening a hotel is a complicated affair, but if you treat it as a mundane occurrence or "just another day at the office," it will not work out very well.

If you feel that life at work has become boring, no matter how complicated it actually is, you must do something to shake it up. That something may be as simple as just taking a holiday to recharge the batteries, or changing direction with your career, or seeking new and different challenges. The beauty of the hospitality industry is that it can offer so many different opportunities, and they are not too hard to find.

Set some new goals. There is always something else to learn, someone else to help. Sit down and examine exactly why you feel as you do. Talk to your loved ones about it. Make some changes in your life. You will soon bounce back.

Tip 98: Turn the other cheek.
Don't bear grudges.

I've had plenty of battles in my career and many of them have finished up in the courts. Some have been nasty. When money is involved, or sometimes, even worse, dented egos, things can get personal. Some people will stop at nothing to get their way, or more likely, to stop you getting yours. I have spent many long hours with senior counsel, trying to figure out whether I will be sued, or whether I should be doing the suing. One thing has become clear to me. In every senior counsel's chambers, there are always rows and rows of books, case histories. In all cases, there is a winner and a loser. What this means is that in every case where counsel's opinion is sought, 50 percent of the opinion seekers will be losers and 50 percent will be winners. And these books are only recording the cases that actually reached the courts. The majority of cases never get that far and settlement is reached out of court long before the case reaches the judge.

Arguments like these, and legal battles, can burn you up; they can take over your life and your very existence. One thing is certain and that is that these things shall pass. Disputes sometimes feel as if they will never end, but they will. When they have, whether you are the lucky winner or the loser, forget them and get on with your life. Don't bear grudges; they will eat you up. Life is too short.

Tip 99: Don't follow the crowd.
You can do it your way.

As I explained, in the opening chapter, I was forced to take on responsibility early in life. I was lucky. Maybe this is why I took a route that was different from the crowd. Maybe I wasn't sure I could get ahead of the crowd or that I would get lost in it. Whatever the reason, it turned out to be the right approach, at least, for me.

It possibly had something to do with sailing, the sport that I loved as a teenager. At every opportunity that presented itself, I took to the water with my little sailboat on one condition—that there was someone else there that I could race. I wasn't particularly successful, but I enjoyed the experience of battling nature, as well as a big fleet of like craft. One fundamental fact about sailboat racing quickly becomes apparent. If another competitor gets ahead of you, you had better get out of his "dirty" air. If you are in the lead in a race, you can enjoy the benefit of clear wind to power your boat along. If that wind has first bounced off the sails of the boat in front of you, it will be disturbed or untrue. It will not power your boat as well as his, and if you pursue the same course as him, you will drop farther and farther behind. If you start at the back of the fleet, which in a way, I believe, I did in the hotel business, you will not get anywhere by following the crowd. You must take a chance and tack for clear water. You must go a different route. Sometimes it will work, and sometimes it won't, but, if you don't try, you won't know.

Sometimes it is easy to believe that there is nothing new under the sun; that all ideas have been tried before. It is not true. And even if it were, you will certainly not have tried them all. I believe America has taught me this too. America is a tonic. It is much ridiculed by Europeans who judge it from soap operas, but it has much to offer. America is a can-do country. Americans don't begrudge others their success; they admire them. Most Americans, however humble their background, believe that they have a chance of success, as is proved by the many who have been successful from lowly beginnings. The "nanny" states of Europe and communism taught people to rely on the state rather than on themselves. People who think this way will always stay in the middle of the fleet. There is something cozy about that. They will, however, never be leaders.

Tip 100: *Keep a balance in life.*
Keep a balance in life.

My children will laugh at this one. I can just hear the talk about the pot calling the kettle black. But after over forty years of marriage, I must have kept some balance in my life, even if Diana had to do most of the balancing. I do, sadly, know of some managers who were not able to do this and, ultimately, made failures of their lives, including their precious jobs.

There is always a reason not to go home in the hotel business. That is because the business never closes and there is always something else to be done. You cannot hang a sign on the door of a hotel at five o'clock saying, "Closed," or another saying, "Sorry, back in five minutes." On the other hand, you cannot do everything by yourself. You need a team and if you never give that team a chance to operate without you, they will never get strong. There are times to go home and give both your subordinates and your family a chance.

All work and no play make *you* dull. If you never take a vacation or develop other interests, you will become one-dimensional. No matter how much you think you are looking after your guests, if you come across as a single-minded, one-dimensional person, you will not be very interesting to them—or to your loved ones. Take time off to enjoy yourself, your friends, and your family. Take an interest in what interests them; it will also make you a more interesting person.

Don't take your work home. On the other hand, don't leave your problems at work. Share them with your partner or loved one. They may not understand all of the nuances or details of the problems, but they can feel them with you, and, maybe, will bring a different insight into situations that could only occur to fresh eyes or to people who know you well. Share with them the excitement of your job; they are entitled to that.

Many years ago, I was approached by Sol Kerzner to work with him for the second time. I promised to go to talk to him but did not tell Diana. That was because I had worked for him before, some ten years earlier, for about ten years and he had been very demanding. So demanding, in fact, that it was very difficult to operate a balanced life. When you worked for Sol, he owned your life. I had determined that I would never work for him again, and I had made, I thought, a reasonable success of working for myself, after I left him. There

was, I discovered, life after Kerzner. Nevertheless, I liked Sol and was curious
as to what he was going to offer me.

Over lunch, he explained what he had in mind. He wanted my help to
build his dream hotel, the Palace of the Lost City, and made me a very attractive offer. I reminded him that we had previously agreed that we could not
work together but that, even if I agreed to try again, this would not be fair to
Diana.

"What if she doesn't mind?" said Sol, ever hopeful.

"Well, then I would consider it," I replied, "but there is not the slightest
possibility that she would want me to do it."

"Well, why don't you ask her?"

With that, I went back to our apartment in London and phoned Diana,
who happened to be in Florida at the time.

"Guess whom I've just seen," I started.

"Sol Kerzner," shot back my psychic wife, "he wants you to work for him,
doesn't he? What did you tell him?"

I then explained what I had said to Sol, and Diana stopped me. "I want you
to know something," she said. "The children and I have often discussed this.
We have all agreed that during the time you were working for Sol, you were
more switched on, alive, energetic, and enthusiastic than before or since. And
this rubbed off onto our lives. I am not saying that our lives have been dull
since then, but we have all agreed that if he ever asks you to work with him
again, you should do it."

I was stunned. I took the job and Diana had been right. I had not realized
how much the positive and negative energy from work had spilled into the
home. Keeping it all bottled up at work would have been a bad and unfair
thing. I thought that I had been a burden on the family at the time; it turns
out that, some of the time, they were enjoying it.

*   *   *

Well, that's it! A century of tips but maybe an inning full of ideas. My original intent in planning this book was to offer a succinct paragraph per tip,
neatly set out, one per page, with plenty of blank spaces—a sort of "One-
Minute Hotel Manager." Alas, I failed. As I thought through each tip, it
seemed to expand, with one idea, dredged from the depths of my experience,
sparking another, and, in turn, leading to yet another, indicating the complex-

ity and interrelationships of all things concerning the management of a business—or more precisely, managing people in business.

So much of our success as managers comes from the touch and feel we develop in organizing and motivating our employees. A single manager cannot look after thousands, or even hundreds, of hotel guests. He relies on the willingness and ability of his employees to get the job done. Each employee, in a day at work, faces hundreds of moments of truth, when the staff interrelate with guests. Every one of these moments can spell danger or success about guest satisfaction. An employee turned off, in some form or another, by negative vibes from his manager will probably fail the test at these moments. That is why so many of my tips are about managing and organizing staff. But they are also about disciplines: the disciplines of budgets, of being in the right place at the right time, of setting stretching goals, of working through check lists, and so on.

The tips are not complicated or difficult to grasp. Taken one by one, they are easy to understand; what is difficult is having the will power, day after day, to translate them all into practice. This book is not a catalog of things every hotel manager should know; it is a blueprint of the more important things a manager should *do!* It is more about action than ideas. On the hierarchy of readers' needs, I hope that I have reached the upper echelons; this book may not be what you expected, but I hope that, in some way, it has been more than you expected and that, as a result, you are, *satisfied?*

Projects the Author Has Been Directly Involved in Designing and/or in Opening and Operating

	Number of rooms
Armani Hotel, Burj Tower, Dubai	320
Armani Hotel, Milan, Italy	120
Atlantis Resort, Paradise Island, Bahamas	2400
Beacon Island Hotel, Plettenberg Bay, RSA	200
Cabana Hotel, Sun City, Bophuthatswana	240
Cap Jaluca Hotel, Anguilla	90
Cape Sun Hotel, Cape Town, RSA	200
Coco Beach Hotel, Mauritius	350
Chobe Game Lodge, Kasane, Botswana	50
Elangeni Hotel, Durban, RSA	450
Great Guana Cay, Bahamas	Cruise ship destination
Hilton Hotel, Munich, Germany	300
Landdrost Hotel, Johannesburg, RSA	240
Malibu Hotel, Durban, RSA	400
Marsa Alam Hotel, Egypt	800
Ocean Club, Paradise Island, Bahamas	100
Palace of the Lost City, South Africa	340
Royal Mirage Hotel, Dubai, UAE	240
Sandton Sun Hotel, Johannesburg, RSA	300
Saint Geran Hotel & Casino, Mauritius	180
Smith and Wollensky, New York, USA	Restaurant
Sonesta Hotel, Milan, Italy	240
Sugar Beach Hotel, Mauritius	240
Sun City Hotel, Bophuthatswana	350
Table Bay Hotel, Cape Town, RSA	300
Touesrock Hotel, Mauritius	200

Projects the Author Was Directly Involved in Complete Renovation and Reopening

Beach Tower, Paradise Island, Bahamas	400
Carlton Tower Hotel, London, UK	320
DeWaal Hotel, Cape Town, RSA	120
Edward Hotel, Durban, RSA	100
Pine Lake Inn, White River, RSA	100
President Hotel, Cape Town, RSA	140
Raffles Night Club Chain, RSA	3 clubs
Ramada Inn, Palm Springs, Calif., USA	180
Ramada Inn, Bakersfield, Calif., USA	180
Royal Swazi Spa, Swaziland	140
Sabie River Bungalows, Kruger Park, RSA	80
Sheraton Hotel, Ithaca, New York, USA	200
Victoria Falls Hotel, Zimbabwe	180

Additional Projects the Author Was Directly Involved in or Responsible for the Management

Beverly Hills Hotel, Durban, RSA	80
Bloemfontein Hotel, Bloemfontein, RSA	120
Blue Marlin Hotel, Natal, RSA	120
BoardWalk Casino, Port Elizabeth, RSA	500 slots
Carnival City Casino, Johannesburg, RSA	1800 slots
Casino Cassis, France	100 slots
Casino Carry-le-Rouet	100 slots
Caino Chamonix	100 slots
Casino Ruhl, Nice, France	340 slots
Cabana Beach Hotel, Durban, RSA	340
Ciskei Sun Casino, Bisho, RSA	250 slots
Elizabeth Hotel, Port Elizabeth, RSA	200
Fish River Hotel and Casino, RSA	150

Gabarone Sun Hotel and Casino, Botswana	200
Galawa Beach Hotel, Moroni, Comores	200
GrandWest Casino, Cape Town, RSA	1800 slots
Harrington Hall Hotel, London, UK	80
Hhluhluwe Game Lodge, Natal, RSA	100
Holiday Inn, Akron, Ohio, USA	180
Holiday Inn, Swaziland	120
Jumers Castle Hotel, Urbana, Ill., USA	140
Kalahari Sands Hotel, Windhoek, Namibia	200
Kimberly Sun Hotel, Kimberly, RSA	120
Lesotho Sun Hotel and Casino, Lesotho	140
Marakesh Casino, Morocco	80 slots
Newlands Hotel, Cape Town, SA	140
Pirogue Hotel, Mauritius	240
Polana Hotel, Maputo, Mozambique	240
Royal Livingstone Hotel, Victoria Falls, Zambia	120
Royale Resorts Holdings, Switzerland	
San Franciscan Hotel, San Francisco, Calif., USA	400
Sonesta Hotel, Milan, Italy	200
Sun International Management, Switzerland	
Sun Vacation, Paris, France	Tour operator
Treasure Cay Hotel and Marina, Bahamas	120
Venda Sun Hotel and Casino	100
Vendome Hotel, Lebanon, Beirut	120
Warwick Hotel, New Orleans, USA	180
World Leisure Tours, Johannesburg, RSA	Tour operator
Zambezi Sun Hotel, Zambia	140
Zimbali Lodge, Durban, SA	80

Author is currently the chairman of Strategic Committee and Investment Committee of Tsogo Sun Holdings, a privately held company with eighty hotels in South Africa, Tanzania, Rwanda, Mozambique, Kenya, Dubai, Seychelles, and five casinos in South Africa with a total of 4,000 slots and 500 gaming tables, *and* chief executive officer of Armani Hotels.

978-0-595-36726-9
0-595-36726-7

CPSIA information can be obtained at www.ICGtesting.com
Printed in the USA
BVOW03s1625240215

389076BV00001B/58/P